LITHGOW

party

paloozas!

52 Unexpected Ways to Make a Birthday, Holiday, or Any Day a Celebration for Kids

John Lithgow

A Broadthink Book

A Lark Production

A FIRESIDE BOOK

PUBLISHED BY SIMON & SCHUSTER

NEW YORK   LONDON   TORONTO   SYDNEY

For my mom, Sarah Lithgow

FIRESIDE
Rockefeller Center
1230 Avenue of the Americas
New York, NY 10020

FIRESIDE and colophon are registered trademarks
of Simon and Schuster, Inc.

For information regarding special discounts
for bulk purchases, please contact
Simon & Schuster Special Sales at 1-800-456-6798
or business@simonandschuster.com

Designed by Charles Kreloff

Manufactured in the United States of America

1 3 5 7 9 10 8 6 4 2

Library of Congress Cataloging-in-Publication Data
Lithgow, John.
Lithgow party paloozas! : 52 unexpected ways to make a birthday, holiday,
or any day a celebration for kids / John Lithgow.
p.   cm.
"A Fireside book."
1. Children's parties—Handbooks, manuals, etc.   2. Amusements—Handbooks, manuals, etc.
3. Games—Handbooks, manuals, etc.   I. Title.
GV1205.L58   2005
793'.21—dc22   2005042536

ISBN 0-7432-7088-6

Acknowledgments

What a bunch of paloozas! A world of thanks to Flynn Berry, Rachel Cagney, Louise Colligan, Jen Park, Maya Stein, and Anna Torres. Big hats off to Elisha Cooper for the gentle fun of his art. A salute to the indefatigable team at Lark, who stoke the creative fires, including Lisa DiMona, Robin Dellabough, and especially Karen Watts. And heartfelt thanks to Nancy Cushing-Jones, Cynthia Cleveland, and Barbara Weller at Broadthink, who just keep egging me on.

Contents

Introduction ix

January Paloozas 1
Baby, It's Cold Outside 2
Latin Lover 7
Sherlock 13
Bubbles! 18
Chinese New Year 24

February Paloozas 29
Dickensia 30
Conversation Hearts 34
Beatlemania 37
Leap! 42

March Paloozas 45
Seasons & Senses 46
Mush! 52
March Hare 57
Sidewalk Café 61

April Paloozas 65
Bonnets & Boxes 66
Opening Day! 69
Mona Lisa 72
One, Two, Tree 77

May Paloozas 83
Tunnels 84

Baby Day 88
Bull Day 91
Sunday in May 98

June Paloozas 103
Deep Blue Sea 104
Stars and Stripes 109
Pops! 114
Superdude 119

July Paloozas 123
T.I.B. 124
Street Games 128
Le Tour 134
Going Mobile 138

August Paloozas 141
True Blue 142
Waterworld 145
Cookin' 150
Inefficiency Day 158
Literary Monsters 162

September Paloozas 167
Checkmate 168
Biopic .171
Gourdgeous 175
Tilting at Windmills 178

October Paloozas 183
Mappa Mundi 184
Dictionary Day 188
It's My Party 191
Teddy 194
Haunted 199

November Paloozas 203
Explorers 204
Monet 208

Alphabet Soup 213
Little Women 217

December Paloozas 221
Wegmania 222
Fly, Baby! 226
Greetings 231
Shortest Day 235
Friday-Night Poker 238

Introduction

Ursula Nordstrom, the great children's book editor, was once asked what made her so good at what she did. She answered, "I was a child once myself, and I haven't forgotten a thing." Paloozas bring together parents and kids by reminding the parents of the things they loved to do when they themselves were kids. In this, my second palooza book, it's all about celebrations and parties.

What's a palooza? It's an invitation to a creative adventure, a little idea that's a great jumping-off point for inventing your own fun. Almost every single day, I see or hear something that makes me think, "Now *that's* a palooza!" That's because every day offers a chance to think and play and flex your imagination. Just look at a calendar. If you're *really* thinking like a palooza, all twelve months of the year are loaded with opportunities to make all new fun. Sure, you can go ahead and celebrate all the familiar holidays and birthdays the way you always have. Or you can turn those days—and every other day—into something special, a real wingding of a palooza!

Make your holidays unique and your birthdays original. Turn your backyard into a water park or your front yard into a snow castle. Celebrate Bubble Day and Leap Year. Celebrate the first day of summer in June and the shortest day of the year in December. Celebrate Frankenstein and Don Quixote and Teddy Roo-

Palooza Key

Each palooza features a sidebar that answers a few key questions about the palooza: Who can play? What do we need? Running time? And what's the budget?

Who can play?

advises age appropriateness. Paloozas are designed for ages ranging from 3 through 12, or for all ages, which means it's great for the whole family.

What do we need?

describes the various materials you might use for the palooza.

Running time?

gives a rough estimate of the time involved to complete the palooza, from a few minutes to an afternoon to a whole weekend.

Budget?

indicates whether the palooza is free, almost free ($), costs just a few dollars ($$), or could cost $20 or more, depending on how many of the suggested materials you have on hand or how all out you want to go on the palooza ($$$). If you're thrifty, you can make lots of these paloozas free or almost free. Use your library as much as you can; it's a gold mine of free palooza resources.

sevelt. And while you're at it, tip your hat to the Eiffel Tower, the Tour de France, and William Wegman and his dogs. Whatever reason you decide to whoop it up, this book offers a nearly endless supply of ideas on how you might do it. Try one of my suggestions on for size, then twist it and bend it and make it your own. *That's* thinking like a palooza!

Many of the ideas in this book you can do for free or almost free, using resources you can find at the library and materials you already have around the house. If you decide to turn the palooza into a full-blown party, it'll cost you about as much as any party costs to put on. As ever, our paloozas involve books, music, food, art, and, of course, the occasional bit of acting. Parents may need to set the stage for the activity, but after that kids are mostly on their own to create, invent, and imagine. You can do them alone, with friends, or with the whole family. And you're certain to find that the more paloozas you play with, the more you'll find to celebrate every single day.

january
paloozas

Baby, It's Cold Outside

Whenever I can, I like to mark the first big snowfall of winter by going outside and making things. Don't look for your usual snowman in my yard, though, unless he happens to be the royal guard in front of my snow castle!

What's the Palooza?

Think of a snow-blanketed park or yard as a giant canvas for all kinds of art and architecture you can create. You can make big pieces intended for public appreciation, or tiny treasures for your own amazement. Get inspiration from your favorite books or music—or straight from the galleries of the finest museums in the world. Try a few of these on for size:

Big Time

There's an incredible oversized earthwork called *Spiral Jetty* on the bed of the Great Salt Lake in Utah. Created by artist Robert Smithson, this 1,500-foot-long, 15-foot-wide coil of basalt rocks was installed in 1970, when the water level of the lake was unusually low. For the last thirty years, the sculpture has been hidden underwater, but periods of drought over the last few years have brought *Spiral Jetty* back into view. Now you can not only see it but, if the water level is low enough, actually walk the length of the salt-encrusted sculpture. The beauty of this piece is in its scale and its audacious use of nature. Have a look at *Spiral Jetty* at www.spiraljetty.org and think about how you might create a gigantic piece like this in the snow.

You can make a spiral like Smithson's or any shape or design out of footsteps (lots of them!) in the snow. What about an Aztec pattern, or a familiar image like artist Keith Haring's barking dog, or a popular icon or logo, like Superman's "S" or the Nike swoosh. Start with a simple sketch of your design on paper, then bundle up and go outside and create an outline of your design with a single set of footsteps to give yourself a plan to follow. Then retrace your steps and begin filling in the design to the size and scale you imagined. Making art this big can be tricky, so step back from time to time (or even better, get a view that looks down on your project) as you work, to check your progress. And try to use most of the space at your disposal to create a dramatic effect—it's your canvas; fill it!

A twist of color can be added to your giant piece by filling spray bottles with water and several drops of food coloring and spritzing it on the snow. Remember, though, that color attracts the heat of the sun and will cause the design to melt sooner than it would if it was left snow-white. Don't forget to take a picture of your big-time art for your scrapbook.

Who can play?
Ages 6 and up.

What do we need?
Snow! Warm clothes (especially well-lined boots and a couple layers of gloves). Food coloring and some spritzing bottles. Lots of half-gallon milk cartons, beach buckets, molds, and sturdy digging tools, like scoops and shovels. Votive candles. A small bucket and a variety of little toys, like action figures, Matchbox cars, or army men.

Running time?
An hour or two, a weekend, or the whole winter!

Budget?
$$

White Castle

I like making castles out of anything—playing cards, cardboard appliance boxes, and sand, of course. Making a winter castle out of snow and ice can be an all-season, entire-neighborhood affair—but that's what makes it so fun.

When the weather drops below freezing and regular snowfall occurs, it's time to begin construction on your mighty snow castle. Start on a weekend or a snow day so you have plenty of time and lots of hands on deck to help. Before your first day of construction, collect as many half-gallon milk or juice cartons as you can, fill them with water, and set them outside overnight to freeze. When you're ready to use, cut away the cartons, and you're left with handy blocks of ice to help fortify your castle.

Grab a few snow shovels and gather any sand-castle-building utensils you have, from buckets and molds to sturdy digging tools like scoops and shovels. Decide where you want to locate your castle; a spot with a little sun is good because it's more pleasant to work and play there. Mark an outline of it with a spritz of water tinted with food coloring or a sprinkle of lawn chalk. Then get your ice blocks, buckets, and molds and start building.

Rome wasn't built in a day, and your snow castle doesn't have to be either. You can make it all winter long if you like, adding height and features as snow and temperature permit. How to keep the blocks of snow or ice from slipping off each other as you stack them? Make a mix of snow and a bit of water in a bucket to create a slush that's good glue for holding pieces together. Professional ice/snow artists call this mixture "sherbet."

Gloves and Other Gear

Anyone who works with snow and ice has a favorite clothing recipe for keeping warm. Most important are head, hands, and feet, and here's a reasonable consensus on how to do it: For the head, a close-fitting natural-fiber cap (cotton or wool), pulled to the eyebrows. Handware needs to allow for some detail work (so big clunky mittens won't do); ice workers swear by cotton jersey gloves worn inside rubber outer gloves (like heavy-duty dishwashing gloves)—this allows for body warmth on the inside and full moisture protection from the outside. Change the inners as needed while you're working. Finally, the boots. Whatever you wear, make sure they're waterproof (moisture is your real enemy, not the cold). Inside, wear two thin layers of winter cotton socks, and, again, change as necessary to stay ahead of any wetness.

The cool tools professional snow and ice artists use are in a league of their own. They include a hatchet, an ice scraper, a small shovel, an ax, rubber gloves, a bucket, and a snow dump. Oh, and an electric chain saw, to make like an arctic Edward Scissorhands, and goggles, so the flying shavings of ice and snow don't get in their eyes!

Finally, pay attention to the time. Even on a sunny day, when it doesn't feel so cold, be careful not to go too long working on your castle without warming up. Every half hour or so, go inside to warm your hands—and keep a spare pair of cotton gloves warming on the radiator to put on when you head outside again.

Snow Lantern

This is easy and beautiful, and you can make one (or a dozen!) every time it snows. Make twenty-five good, solid, round snowballs, each at least the size of a baseball. Arrange ten of them in a circle, each snowball touching the other firmly but not smashed tightly together (you need a little bit of air between the snowballs so your lantern can "breathe"). Set a votive candle (or a slightly larger-sized candle) in the middle of the circle. Arrange the next eight in a circle on top of the ten, then six on top of the eight, working to make a cone shape that will come to a point. Add the next four, then reach in with a long fireplace match to light your candle (make sure a grown-up is supervising or assisting). Top the opening with one last snowball, and enjoy the gentle glow of your snow lantern.

If you're having a holiday party, make a few of these lanterns to decorate your porch or sidewalk. And don't forget to blow out the candles when the festivities wind down.

Ice Frieze

Take a tall plastic container (like a deli container) and fill it with water. Set it outside on an icy day and watch for when it begins to freeze. When you see it begin to thicken (like Jell-O does in the fridge), drop in an action figure or two or a small car or plastic toy, and let it set outside overnight. The next day, turn the container over onto a plastic plate and shake it until the ice jiggles

Arctic Architecture

Maybe the most extreme polar-style vacation destination in the world is the Mammut Snow Hotel in the Kemi region of Lapland, Finland, just below the Arctic Circle. This is a snow castle right from someone's wild imagination, with turrets, battlements, and a drawbridge—and illuminated with lanterns that bring it to life. There are several buildings that make up the hotel, including seventeen guest rooms (kept at a comfortable -5° C with polar sleeping bags for bedgear, of course) and a restaurant consisting of long tables and benches made of ice and fitted with reindeer skins, candles, and Lappish cuisine. There's also an ice chapel and Children's World, a snowy white playground with tunnels, hills, and slides. Mammut is open from December 31 to the first week of April. Go to www.snowcastle.net to have a look at these one-of-a-kind accommodations.

free. You can enjoy your little stop-action ice scene as is, or noodle with the shape of the ice form with simple ice-carving tools like a Phillips or flathead screwdriver, hammer, and metal file to round it out like a snow globe. Work with gloves on, of course, to protect your fingers while working with the tools.

Photo Finish

Some of the prettiest outdoor pictures you can take (especially using black-and-white film) are during the snowiest, iciest bits of winter. During those ultra-quiet moments just after a snowstorm or ice storm, or when the sun turns up for the big meltdown after a storm, grab a camera, go outside, and get some money shots. Trees loaded down with snow or encased in ice, a giant icicle hanging from the gutter outside your bedroom window, or something as simple as a bootprint or snow angel impressed on new snow—there's no end to photographic subjects in winter. The great American landscape photographer Ansel Adams relished the frosting of winter on some of his favorite subjects. A great example is *Fresh Snow,* taken in Yosemite Valley in 1947; go to www.anseladams.com to have a look at his photos of nature in winter, snow, and ice.

Latin Lover

I love Cicero for his passion for politics and philosophy, language and leisure. In a single day, he could give a fierce speech on the floor of the Roman Senate, engage in a dangerous round or two of cloakroom intrigue, translate a passage of Socrates from Greek to Latin, write a brilliant letter to a friend, attend the theater, and pass a peaceful hour reading or puttering in his garden. *That's* living.

What's the Palooza?

To Cicero and other ancient Romans, the quality of life was measured by the quality of their leisure. They believed that leisure was as important as labor, but the Romans were no slackers! They worked hard so they could fully enjoy their free time playing games, indulging in long debates or meals, or attending fabulous public spectacles like the Circus Maximus, which featured chariot races and other wild contests.

Follow a cue from Cicero and company and make time for simple pleasures, Roman-style! Play games, make toys, write letters, have a feast. The ancients (young and old) were very fond of games like handball *(expulsim ludere)*, trigon, soccer, field hockey, *harpasta, phaininda, episkyros,* catch, and a form of dodgeball.

Who can play?
Ages 9 and up.

What do we need?
A kickball or dodgeball for trigon and pila games; nice paper and a fancy pen for letter writing and maxims.

Running time?
Anywhere from twenty minutes to two hours, depending on how Roman you want to go.

Budget?
$$

Trigon

Winning this game depends on your style and skill in "faking out" other players. Position three players *(trigonalias)* in a triangle, about twenty feet apart. Throw a baseball or softball, left-handed, to the player on the right, who then catches the ball in his left hand and

Cicero was born on January 3, 106 B.C.

How to Tie a Toga

Drape a long end of an old flat bedsheet from back to front over one shoulder. Take the other end of the sheet in the opposite hand and drape it across your chest and over the same shoulder from front to back. To prevent a droopy drape, you can tie the top end in a knot over the underlayer. Or cheat a little and fasten a large safety pin just behind your shoulder.

passes it to the third player, and so on. Volley counter-clockwise continuously until a player decides to switch directions, either batting the ball to the left with his right hand or to the right with his left hand. If a catch-able ball is dropped or missed, the thrower gets a point; the first person to reach 21 points is the winner. The *pilecripus* (scorekeeper) may return a dropped ball to the *trigonalia* who dropped it. Skillful players may even introduce a second ball.

Pila

This game is a little like monkey-in-the-middle, played with a kickball-sized ball. Arrange four to ten players standing in a wide circle, with one additional player, the middle runner *(medius currens),* inside the circle. Throw the ball across the player next to you to any nonadjacent player, while the middle runner tries to intercept it. If the play is obstructed, the thrower becomes the middle runner. If the ball is dropped, the player losing the ball becomes the middle runner.

Troy

Troy, or *lusus Troiae,* was a rough-and-tumble game where the kid who was It had to resist a gang of opponents trying to capture him by dragging him across a battle line. Yikes, maybe a little too rough! Invent your own game of Troy that involves teams and sneaky strategies for capturing opponents. Maybe it's a kind of battlefield version of flag football, each player with a team-colored scarf tucked into his pants for snatch/capture. Break into two teams, then maybe into smaller units of one or two people within the teams, depending on how many kids are playing. Establish two "encampments" where opposing team members are taken when captured. Determine your playing field—that is, the exact boundaries of land within which players can move to advance strategies or avoid capture. Make up your own simple rules; maybe everyone has to keep moving—no hiding or stalling in one spot for more than one minute at a time. The fun in your game of Troy should be creating rules that make the game challenging and working out strategies for capturing or eluding opposing players.

Knucklebones!

The Romans loved the game of knucklebones, which is like our game of jacks, only played with bones. Create your own version of knucklebones using a beanbag or tennis ball and twelve to twenty items to drop and collect

Make It a Party!

The Romans were famous for their elaborate feasts, which sometimes continued for eight to ten hours and featured musicians, dancers, and poets, in addition to a parade of elaborate dishes. Turn your home into a Roman banquet hall and throw your own bash, complete with Roman-style food, games, and togas.

Invites: Tea-stained or parchment paper cut into a tablet shape. In your best blocky hand lettering, begin, "Friends, Romans, countrymen . . . Come to a party!" followed by the party date—in Roman numerals, of course.

Costumes: All you need for costumes are bedsheet togas, sandals, and a leafy homemade wreath. Wear a comfy T-shirt and sweats underneath your toga.

Food and Decor: Strew pillows on the floor and drape sheets over doorways. If you have a low couch or chairs, invite guests to recline while eating, as the nobles did. (Only slaves ate sitting up.) Make architectural columns out of large cardboard tubes, painted and decorated with a flourish. Fill a basin or large bowl with water for guests to wash their hands in before the meal. Serve grapes, olives, figs, cheese, bread with olive oil for dipping and crackers. Present sparkling fruit juice in plastic goblets (available at party stores).

Activities: Play Roman games. Make a knucklebones game. Watch *Spartacus*, *Ben-Hur*, or another classical favorite.

Favors: Small gift bags full of figs, nuts, and Roman (chocolate) coins.

with each throw of the ball. Pencils, bottle caps, barrettes, plastic spoons—almost anything pick-up-able will do (coins or keys could be tricky because they fall flat and don't pick up easily). Use all similar items or mix them up to create a unique pick-up challenge. Make your own rules involving the number of items to be picked up, or what constitutes a valid ball toss, or what it takes to win. However your game goes, it'll require a quick eye and good reflexes to be a knucklebones champ.

Epistolary Pen Pals

Cicero was famous for his correspondence, a vast collection of letters he wrote to friends, filled not with idle chatter but with thoughtful explanations of ideas that were important to him. More than two thousand years later, we still have access to hundreds of his letters on subjects as varied as politics, old age, the nature of the gods, and good behavior. These letters are historical artifacts that reflect the workings of a sharp and curious mind, and reveal a lot about the details of day-to-day Roman life and culture.

When in Rome . . .

Whoever said Latin is a dead language hasn't been to Latin Summer Camp in Rome *(Aestiva Romae Latinitatis)*, which is taught by Father Reginald Foster, an American-born priest and monk who works at the Vatican and is known as "the Pope's Latinist." Students in Father Reggie's demanding, tuition-free program translate articles from the morning newspaper into Latin, discuss philosophy in Latin *sub arboribus* (outside under the trees), and roam around Rome reading Cicero near the places he describes in his writings. Or skip going to Rome and download Father Reggie's lectures and homework assignments from www.geocities.com/frcoulter/latin.html and teach yourself Latin right from home!

Bring back the lost art of letter writing—begin a letter-writing relationship with someone you know and become the *literati illuminati* of your own age! The ideal pen pal can be a relative or friend, anyone with whom you'd feel comfortable sharing your thoughts and opinions. Choose a subject or subjects that you're keenly interested in (sports, horses, music) or write about your opinion on things that are happening in the world. Keep your style crisp and your meaning clear—Cicero had no patience for sloppy or boring use of language. Consider the letters you send and receive in return as a kind of conversation that requires both of you to search for the right words to express what you think. And save your letters in a shoe box or portfolio! The best letter writers in history always kept their correspondence.

Maximum Maxims

Cicero was a master of summing up his grand philosophies of life in one sentence. Here are a few of his many memorable maxims:

A friend is a second self.

It is not enough to have wisdom; you must know how to use it.

Peace is freedom in tranquillity.

What sweetness is left in life, if you take away friendship? Robbing life of friendship is like robbing the world of the sun.

By doubting, we all come at truth.

Friendship improves happiness and relieves misery, by doubling our joy and dividing our grief.

As an exercise in style, try your hand at writing Ciceronian epigraphs.

New Words for a New World

When Cicero decided to translate the works of the great Greek philosophers into Latin, he meant to bring important ideas from the old civilization to the new center of the world. In the process, though, he did for Latin what Chaucer did for English: he helped to establish the language by inventing useful new Latin words to express Greek concepts. Some of his word creations included the Latin for words like *morals, property, individual, science, image,* and *appetite.* Can you imagine our modern society without a word for science or property? He wasn't just creating words for the sake of creating words; he was inventing new words for new concepts that would help advance his culture.

Invent an all-new word to describe an experience that is brand-new to you: What an oyster tastes like. What a kitten looks like when it's being born. What a waterfall smells like. Don't use words you already know to describe a new experience; make a new word out of bits and pieces of other words, sounds-like phonetic combinations, or just letters you're fond of. Use your new word with confidence . . . then see if you overhear someone else using your contribution to the language!

Sherlock

What do the Baker Street Irregulars of London have in common with the Red Circle of Niigala, Japan, and the Persian Slipper Club of San Francisco? They are all official groups of Sherlock Holmes fanatics. These clubs challenge their members to write and solve mysteries, complete puzzles, play detective games, and occasionally wear double-brimmed deerstalker hats à la Sherlock Holmes. This palooza turns your home into 221B Baker Street.

What's the Palooza?

The palooza is elementary, my dear Watson. Write a mini-mystery in the style of Sir Arthur Conan Doyle. Start by dipping into a few of Doyle's stories featuring the world-famous fictional detective Sherlock Holmes. From the collection *The Adventures of Sherlock Holmes,* you might read the short stories "The Red-Headed League," "The Blue Carbuncle," and "The Speckled Band." He wrote fifty-six short stories in all, as well as four novels, the most popular probably being *The Hound of the Baskervilles.* Read any or all of them, and you'll be "up to snuff" on Sherlock's crime-solving style.

Dr. Watson was Sherlock's associate and friend, a true partner in detection. He was also the narrator of the stories, so all is revealed through his telling. Create your own pair of sleuths in the Holmes/Watson spirit. Develop one protagonist as a debonair, witty problem solver many paces ahead of his Watson, a character full of obvious questions and wrong deductions, and a narrator capable of insightful observations that help engage the reader in the story. Give them splendid names and colorful backstories. Outfit them in dashing attire and intriguing props.

Who can play?
Ages 9 and up.

What do we need?
Sherlock Holmes short stories, notebook, and writing materials; Sherlock Holmes videos.

Running time?
A few hours.

Budget?
Free.

Detective Sherlock Holmes was born on January 6, 1854.

By a man's finger-nails, by his coat-sleeve, by his boots, by his trouser-knees, by the callosities of his forefinger and thumb, by his expression, by his shirt-cuffs—by each of these things a man's calling is plainly revealed. That all united should fail to enlighten the competent inquirer in any case is almost inconceivable.

—Sherlock Holmes, in "A Study in Scarlet"

Next, decide on the crime and present it forthwith—something or someone is missing; someone has been harmed in some way, perhaps, dare we say it, mysteriously murdered. Get your sleuths to the scene of the crime ASAP so they can make a careful examination of the facts of the case. Include in your description of the crime scene both ordinary and unusual clues, thus giving your sleuths an opportunity to interact in the Sherlock/Watson style.

Introduce your suspects. Do ensure that at least one of them, your true culprit, tells an actual lie that doesn't seem like a lie and that others under suspicion tell truths that seem like lies. Do they have something in common with each other that your detectives—and the reader—need to figure out?

Holmesiana

There are hundreds of Sherlock Holmes clubs around the world, and many more Web sites and books by and for the detective's devout fans. Some of the best resources to explore for your own interest in Sherlock Holmes include www.221bakerstreet.org, where you can access the complete text of forty-eight of the sixty Holmes stories by Sir Arthur Conan Doyle. Go to www.bakerstreet221b.de/canon/6houn.htm to download a terrific facsimile of the original edition of *The Hound of the Baskervilles,* including all sixty original illustrations that accompanied the text. The Bantam Classics edition of *The Complete Sherlock Holmes* features all sixty stories between two covers. Other fun books for Sherlock lovers are *The Baker Street Companion,* by Paul Lipari, and *The Bedside, Bathtub and Armchair Companion to Sherlock Holmes,* by Dick Riley and Pam McAllister. Be sure to rent the 1939 film version of *The Hound of the Baskervilles,* starring Basil Rathbone and Nigel Bruce, as well as any of the other thirteen movies made between 1939 and 1946 featuring the Sherlock Holmes character. Finally, rent *Young Sherlock Holmes* for the fun of imagining a young Holmes and Watson solving their first mystery at the boarding school they attend.

Bring the threads of your story together with a cliffhanger, where you have gathered the appropriate people for a confrontation and your hero presents the clues and his final deduction as to the true culprit. Perhaps there's a bit of a scuffle at the end, as the culprit tries to escape. Or maybe there's a confession. Sew it up with a final conversation between your two detectives.

Read your detective story aloud—or perform it as a play—before an audience of friends or family. Invite them to solve the mystery before you reveal the solution at the end.

Powers of Observation

Among Sherlock Holmes's many gifts are his great powers of observation. Honing such skill takes training. To work on yours, walk into a room and take a sixty-second look at a particular area, say the desk or kitchen counter. Leave the room and write down all the items you remember seeing, then return to the room to see what you missed. Try the same exercise, only enter a room and try to take a mental account of the whole room—there's a red couch with two throw pillows on it, a coffee table with three magazines, a side table with a book, telephone, and ballpoint pen. Some of these things you'll remember because they're so familiar to you; who could forget they have a red couch in their living room? But the other stuff is kind of invisible to you until you start to flex your observation muscles. Continue to improve your eye by making a sixty-second study of scenes outside your home. Say you're at the grocery store. How many people were in line with you at the checkout? How many were men, how many were women? What were they buying? The more you practice taking in small scenes, the better your ability to notice little details that might be important—especially for your fictional detective!

Where's Sherlock When You Need Him?

In the 1920s Sir Arthur Conan Doyle was among the many people taken in by two young English girls, ages sixteen and ten, who perpetuated the Cottlinger Fairies Hoax for years. The girls reported that they had been visited by fairies while playing in the woods. Their evidence? Photographs they took of fairies who seemed to be flying about the girls' heads. Many people, including Doyle and magician Harry Houdini, completely believed that the photographs were genuine, not doctored. Doyle wrote about this incident and supported the girls' claims to the existence of the fairies until they confessed to the hoax years later. The fairies turned out to be not evidence that would stand up to the scrutiny of a Sherlock Holmes, but evidence of the girls' imaginations and their skills with paper, scissors, and a camera!

Witness

With notebook in hand, park yourself in a good people-watching zone and work on being the perfect witness. A library or a bookstore with seating would work, or you can even do it on the school bus. Choose two or three people on which to do a "witness workup." Try to take in as many details about the person as possible: gender, height, coloring, clothing, accessories, details of their behavior. Do they wear glasses or carry a backpack? What are they reading? Working on being a good witness will make the details of your own detective story much more interesting and believable. And you might even think of a way to use some version of the people you observe as characters in your story.

Bubbles!

Bubbles are like popcorn—irresistible, giggly, and just plain fun. Thank heavens someone had the presence of mind to mark a day on the calendar to remind us.

What's the Palooza?

This is a party, straight up, all bubbles and nothing but fun.

A Bubble You

Before the party, lay four-foot-long strips of bubble wrap out flat, one per guest. When guests arrive, have them lie down on the strips of bubble wrap and outline their bodies with a Sharpie marker. Cut out the bubble children, like big bubble-wrap paper dolls. Then create self-portraits, using the bubble cutouts as the basic canvas. Use quick-drying paint and/or offer a variety of felt or fabric cutout features (like eyes, noses, mouths, ears) to glue on the figure. Glue on ribbons, yarn, scraps of cloth, felt, colored construction or tissue paper, and sparkles to make one-of-a-kind bubble self-portraits—realistic or out of this world—to take home.

Frozen Bubbles

National Bubble Day is January 8.

This is a quickie you create at the beginning of your party, then ooh and aah over at the end. You just need small paper plates, bubble solution and wand, and room enough in your freezer to stow the plates. Write your name on a small paper plate. Choose the designated bubble blower (a grown-up would be best, so as to minimize the chances of slick and slippery bubble residue ending up on the floor). As the bubble blower blows bubbles, try to catch one or two on your paper plate, one party guest at a time. Gently (and rather quickly) place your plate in the freezer. Check in on your frozen bubbles at the end of the party. Cool!

Bubble Couture

Design an outfit with bubble wrap. Make dresses, togas, vests, hats, pants, skirts, or capes with bubble wrap. Arrange the bubble wrap into the shape of a piece of clothing (just like using cloth, but bubblier) and decorate your outfit to wear during the party. Use old neckties, costume jewelry, feathers, ribbons, and large sequins to glue on, tie up, or decorate your creations. Use glue sparingly so it will dry quickly. Write a bubble poem while the glue dries, put on your outfits, and have a fashion show. Lots of paparazzi photos, please!

Bubble Poem

In advance of the party, cut twenty or thirty different-sized circles out of colored construction paper. Guests sitting on the floor in a half-circle take turns thinking of words that describe bubbles—what they look like, feel like, sound like, taste like, where you find them, and so on. Collect the words on a notepad, then copy each onto a colored circle. Spread the words on the floor so everyone can see them. Move the words around to suggest different combinations to make a poem. Some of the words might be *fizzy, tickle, surprise,*

Who can play?
Ages 3–6.

What do we need?
Loads of bubble wrap (available at office supply stores or shipping centers), quick-drying tempera or poster paint and brushes, cloth and felt scraps, tissue paper, sparkles, sequins, buttons, feathers, neckties, play jewelry, and glue. More bubble wrap, blue painter's tape, string, paint, or glue-on scraps. Bubble solution and small paper plates. Tempera paint, large plastic cups, more bubble solution, and sturdy white construction paper. Poster board, colored cellophane, tape, and markers. Camera.

Running time?
Two hours.

Budget?
$$$

and *pop,* and a little bubble poem using those words
might be:

*A fizzy bubble tickles
And pop-pop-pops against my tongue
Like a surprise party inside my mouth.*

Glue or tape the bubble poem words to a piece of poster
board, writing the connecting words between the bubbles with a Sharpie. Don't forget to give your poem a
title. This one might be called "A Sip of Soda"!

Bubble Art

Set up a generous spread of newspapers on the kitchen
floor or other work surface. Mix 1 to 2 teaspoons of different colors of tempera or poster paint (or 8–10 drops of
food coloring) into individual cups of bubble solution.
Use a straw to gently blow into the cups until bubbles
flow over the top. Lay a piece of white paper gently on

Make It a Party!

- - - - - - -

Invites: Decorate cards or paper with a bubble border for the invitations. "Join us for a
bubble of a time at Jimmy's bubble-rific Fifth Birthday. . . ."

Food and Decor: All foods round or bubbly—multicolored melon balls, Swedish meatballs
and gravy or Italian rice balls and marinara sauce, Bubble Bread, and ice cream sodas!
Decorate with lots of clear balloons hanging from the ceiling or floating to the ceiling (if
filled with helium) to look like giant bubbles. Use bubble wrap to cover the party-table
chairs so kids can sit on bubble thrones.

Favors: Store-bought bottles of bubbles, covered with a homemade label: "Jimmy's Bubble-rific Fifth Birthday." Affix the labels by taping over them with wide, clear packing tape
so that the words don't run when they get covered with bubble solution. Blow Pops.
Bazooka Joe. A souvenir photo of each guest in his bubble outfit and/or blowing a bubble
in the bubble-blowing contest. Decorate oversize plastic cups with permanent marker with
day and date of the party . . . and lots of bubbles, of course. Stow goodies in the cup,
along with a super-sipping crazy straw.

How to Blow a Bubble-Gum Bubble

Bubble-gum lovers have loads of opinions about what makes for the best bubble-gum bubbles. To start with, most agree you should avoid the big, soft, brightly flavored brands like Bubble Yum or Bubblicious if you want to blow big bubbles. Old-timey brands like Bazooka Joe or Double Bubble are better. Here are some tips for blowing big bubbles: One or two pieces of gum is plenty. More isn't better when it comes to blowing bubbles. Blow your bubbles indoors. Heat or cold, as well as wind, are no good for bubbles. Chew your gum for up to five minutes to get it warmed up for blowing. Now flatten the gum between your tongue and your front teeth. Open your mouth a bit and use your tongue to start pushing a bubble out between your teeth. Blow out gently until a bubble starts to take shape. The trick to blowing a big bubble is to blow s-l-o-w-l-y, to give the gum time to stretch evenly. And keep your mouth open a little all the while you're blowing, to give it plenty of air for steady inflation.

top of the cup until several bubbles pop, and then lift off carefully. The paper captures the colored impression of the bubbles when they pop. Let each color of bubbles dry before you move on to another color. By the time you're done, you'll have a bubbly bit of psychedelic pop art!

Bubble-Blowing Contest

Using either bubble solution and wand or bubble gum (or both!) have a bubble blowing contest. Every guest gets three tries; whoever blows the biggest bubble wins. A Mr. Bubble product would be a good prize.

Bash the Bubble Monster

This is just like pounding on a piñata, only it's beating the sweet stuffings out of a monster made of bubble wrap who's loaded in his nooks and crannies with candies and trinkety treats. In advance of the party, take a roll of bubble wrap and any scraps of wrap you have saved from your various shipping experiences. To create the monster's body, take a length of bubble wrap and roll a big ol' cylinder, adding small candies and treats in the first couple of rolls. Tape the body lengthwise with painter's tape (not too tightly, or it might be difficult to "liberate" the candies come monster-bashing time). Tie a piece of string around the top and bottom of the cylinder, Tootsie Roll style. Roll shorter, thinner cylinders for the arms and legs, again tucking in candies as you roll and tying each at both ends with string. To create the head, take an oversize square of bubble wrap (18 by 18 inches), lay a good supply of candy and

Bubble Bread

Bread
1 cup sugar
2 tablespoons cinnamon
4-pack of plain or buttermilk refrigerated biscuit tubes (7.5 ounces each)

Topping
1 stick butter or margarine, melted
3/4 cup brown sugar
Powdered sugar optional

Preheat oven to 350°. Combine sugar and 1 teaspoon cinnamon in a large ziplock bag. Cut each biscuit into 4 pieces, roll into balls, and add to the bag with the cinnamon sugar mixture. Shake well to coat. Place biscuit pieces into a bundt cake pan that has been lightly coated with cooking spray.

Combine topping ingredients in a mixing bowl and pour over biscuits. Bake for 23 to 28 minutes. Remove from the oven and let cool slightly before loosening the edges of the bread gently with a knife. Let cool for at least 10 to 15 minutes, then place a large plate upside down on top of the pan and flip the bread over onto the plate. Sprinkle with a little powdered sugar, if you like. Stick some candles in the bread for "Happy Birthday," then remove the candles and have guests pull off their own sweet pieces of bubble bread.

treats in the center, gather the edges together in your fist like a sack, then tie securely with string. Use painter's tape to attach arms and legs to the body, and use another length of string or tape to attach the head. Shake him a little like a rag doll to be sure he's attached securely enough to give the little sluggers a bit of a challenge. Reinforce with string or painter's tape as necessary. Give your monster crazy hair by attaching different lengths of yarn to the sticky side of a bit of packing tape, then secure it with another piece of tape, sticky face down, to its head. Paint a face on the head (or glue scraps of fabric or felt for facial features) as well as an appropriately monsterish outfit. When it's dry and ready to go, attach a rope or wire to the monster by the neck for hanging from an appropriate spot, preferably outdoors. Come end-of-party time, everyone takes a whack with a wiffle ball bat until he falls, and the usual piñata-style free-grab for candy ensues. Besides the sweet treats, the guests are offered a free pass to pop the monster's bubble-wrap bubbles without a grown-up saying, "Stop already!"

Bubbletalk

Try to guess what these words or phrases mean. And if you don't know, take a crazy guess!

Bubble and squeak

Bubble chamber

Bubble dance

Bubble over

Bubble pack

Bubble shell

Bubble up

Bubblejet

Bubbler

Bubbling

Bubbly

Chinese New Year

In New York, Chinese New Year lights the neighborhood of China-town on fire with color and life in the coldest part of winter. The streets come alive with fabulous dragons and graceful dancers dressed in red and gold. On the street and in the home, this holiday honors family, past and present. Join in the spirit of the Chinese New Year—or adapt the vibrant traditions for your own family festivities.

Who can play?

All ages can partici-pate; adult supervision needed for cooking and crafts.

What do we need?

Plants and oranges, smocks or robes, green or black loose tea, materials for crafts (see below), and ingre-dients for recipes (see below).

Running time?

Two to three hours.

Budget?

$$

What's the Palooza?

Chinese New Year begins with the new moon on the first day of the new year and ends on the full moon fifteen days later. It is the biggest holiday in China and has been a central part of Chinese culture for millennia. Preparations for New Year's day last about a month and are full of the best kind of hustle and bustle: buying presents, filling the house with fresh flowers and plants, and even giving the door a fresh coat of red paint to welcome in the new year. New Year's Eve and New Year's Day are celebrated with the whole family—includ-ing ancient ancestors! Families prepare a dinner for the family ancestors on New Year's Eve so their spirits can cheer the new year along with the family.

Out with the Old, In with the New

Before New Year's Day, Chinese families start by giving their homes a good cleaning. Call it the Big Sweep; the

Chinese believe a house should be spotless on New Year's Day to welcome in a fresh year, and so they sweep away the previous year's bad luck with a broom. Next they adorn their houses with blooming flowers and plants, bowls of fruit, and trays of candy. All of the decorations have a deeper meaning than just decoration: plants symbolize rebirth, and a flower that blooms on New Year's Day promises a year of success, while oranges and tangerines represent happiness. The Chinese also hang good wishes written on red paper on walls and doors. Express wishes like "May you enjoy good fortune" and "May you be blessed with abundant love" by writing them on sturdy drawing paper and hanging them about the house. Use sticky tack to pin them to the wall.

Chinese New Year is on or about January 24.

Dress for Success

The Chinese wear clothing on the New Year that is beautiful and rich, with lush fabrics and vibrant colors, to reflect the wearer's hopes and set the tone for the new year. Bright red clothing is favored because it is thought to set the stage for a bright and happy future. You can look your best in a simple Chinese-style outfit, based on the traditional cheongsam. A cheongsam is usually brocade or silk, embroidered with lucky patterns, such as symbols for health and prosperity. Make your own cheongsam out of a nightgown with a red sash tied around the waist, or pajama pants topped with a long tunic or collared shirt.

Do-It-Yourself Dragon

You want your house to be as colorful and merry as possible, so start by making a Chinese New Year dragon out of paper egg cartons, scissors, a hole punch, red, yellow and black craft paint, a paintbrush, ribbon (about $1/4$-inch wide), tacky glue, a pair of googly eyes, $1/4$-inch white pom-pom balls, and a half-inch jingle

Chinese Zodiac

You might know if you are an Aries or Virgo, but do you know your Chinese zodiac sign? The Chinese lunar New Year is based on a cycle of twelve years: it begins with the rat and ends with the boar before starting over again. The names for each year come from an ancient legend. In the myth, Lord Buddha summoned all the animals to visit him before he left the earth. Only twelve animals came to pay their respects and send him off, and as a reward for their loyalty, he named a year after each one in the order they arrived. The Chinese believe the animal ruling the year in which you are born has enormous impact on your personality. Does your year fit you?

Rat   1924   1936   1948   1960   1972   1984   1996
Rats are creative, charming, and loving.

Ox   1925   1937   1949   1961   1973   1985   1997
Oxen are confident, demanding, and influential.

Tiger   1926   1938   1950   1962   1974   1986   1998
Tigers are bold, adventurous, and love taking risks.

Rabbit   1927   1939   1951   1963   1975   1987   1999
Rabbits are friendly, easygoing, and affectionate.

Dragon   1928   1940   1952   1964   1976   1988   2000
Dragons are popular, lively, and enthusiastic.

Snake   1929   1941   1953   1965   1977   1989   2001
Snakes are romantic, wise, and contemplative.

Horse   1930   1942   1954   1966   1978   1990   2002
Horses are hardworking, independent, and resourceful.

Sheep   1931   1943   1955   1967   1979   1991   2003
Sheep are elegant, artistic, and free-spirited.

Monkey   1932   1944   1956   1968   1980   1992   2004
Monkeys are admired, intelligent, and successful.

Rooster   1933   1945   1957   1969   1981   1993   2005
Roosters are diligent, decisive, and outspoken.

Dog   1934   1946   1958   1970   1982   1994   2006
Dogs are honest, conscientious, and loyal.

Boar   1935   1947   1959   1971   1983   1995   2007
Boars are tolerant, honest, and make great friends.

bell. Don't worry if you're missing the last four items; you can simply make eyes for your dragon with markers or colors you do have. Cut the cups of the egg carton apart. Even out the edges so each cup will sit solidly upside down on the table. Paint the inside of one cup black for the inside of the mouth. Paint the outside yellow. Using as few or as many cups as you wish, paint the outside of the remaining cups yellow. Let dry. Paint different-colored dots on the yellow cups. Let dry. Hole-punch two holes on the sides of each cup, directly across from each other. Lace the ribbon through the holes to tie the dragon together, making sure your special headpiece is last on one end. (The head is attached through a single hole punched in the top of the cup.) Leave an inch or so of ribbon after the final knot is tied to serve as the dragon's tongue. Tie a jingle bell on the tail end of the ribbon. Then glue two googly eyes to the pom-poms and let them dry. Then glue the pom-poms to the top of the head.

Fortune Teller

Chinese New Year is based around ancient rituals and superstitions. Get into the spirit by reading tea leaves to tell your fortune! Brew a pot of loose green or black tea (ask an adult for help as necessary). Drink your tea slowly until there is a small amount of tea left at the bottom of the cup. Swirl the cup three times and turn the cup upside down to drain the tea. Now turn your cup over. What do you see? The leaves closer to the rim will tell the near future, while the leaves down in the base of the cup tell of the distant future. Find pictures in the leaves, like you do while looking at clouds. Here are what some images indicate may be on the horizon:

bells: good news
chain: success but with effort
fish: news or travel abroad

key: the solving of a mystery
egg: fertility
flowers: love
spider: luck

Cook Up a Great Year

Chinese New Year celebrations overflow with delicious food. In hopes of securing abundance and wealth in the new year, the Chinese load dinner tables with wonton soup, pot stickers, noodles, and egg rolls. Try this simple good-fortune-boosting dessert:

Nian Gao (Chinese New Year's Cakes)

There are many different types of New Year's cakes; some have dates, some peanuts. Ours are coated in sesame seeds.

$2^1/_2$ cups packed dark brown sugar
$^1/_2$ cup vegetable oil
$4^1/_2$ cups sweet rice flour (glutinous flour), found in
    Asian markets
2 teaspoons baking powder
$^1/_2$ teaspoon salt
sesame seeds

Heat the brown sugar and the vegetable oil together in a sauté pan; stir constantly, until sugar melts, then cool slightly. In a bowl, combine the flour, baking powder, and salt. Stir cooled brown sugar mixture into the flour. Drop the batter by the spoonful into a bowl of sesame seeds. Coat completely then place balls into a steamer, then cover and steam for 50–60 minutes.

Sometimes the chef puts a coin or tiny treasure into one of the cakes: whoever finds the treat is sure of a particularly good year to come!

february
paloozas

Dickensia

I once came upon a cheerful, energetic young woman named Polly Golucky, who made me think immediately of Charles Dickens. I'm sure he'd know what to do with a name like that.

Who can play?
Ages 6 and up.

What do we need?
Thesaurus, baby name book, or Internet access to an online thesaurus, paper and pencil, age-appropriate books by Dickens, such as *Oliver Twist, David Copperfield,* or *A Christmas Carol.*

Running time?
An hour or more.

Budget?
Free.

Charles Dickens's birthday is February 7, 1812.

What's the Palooza?

Charles Dickens was a literary rock star in nineteenth-century England, a hugely popular novelist whose stories were eagerly read in weekly installments first published in newspapers and magazines, then published later as whole books. Because his stories were published in pieces, or *serialized,* the chapters tended to end with a bit of tension, like a mini-cliffhanger, so that the readers would be anxious to read the next installment and find out what happened next. His stories were also loaded with vivid characters, good and bad, who had exaggerated features and memorable characteristics that made them easy for the reader to identify from one installment to the next. And quite often, a character's most exaggerated feature was his or her name.

Dickens's characters' names were often made up of suggestive sounds or the hint of a pun that were clues to the nature of the character. In *Great Expectations,* for instance, you find Pip, the little seedling of a boy who will take the long way around growing into a wise, mature man. There's Estella, the glimmering and unattainable young woman whose love stays just outside Pip's reach. There's Magwitch, the fearsome escaped convict who scares the dickens (!) out of Pip at the beginning of the story, and later causes the mysterious improvement of Pip's fortunes. There's Jaggers, Magwitch's frightful and intimidating lawyer. And there's Dolge Orwick, the nasty blacksmith's assistant who nearly kills Pip.

Based just on their names—Betsy Prig, Seth Pecksniff, Mrs. Crummles, Polly Toodles, Jenny Wren, Chevy Slyme, or Wackford Squeers—what do you think these Dickens characters might be like? Do you think you'd have fun at the school where Mr. M'Choakumchild is the headmaster? You get the idea. Now invent some of your own Dickensian-style names, and colorful characters to go with them.

The Name Game

To play the Dickensian name game, start by practicing on your own family. Think about a distinguishing trait

Meet the Neighbors

Dickens had a brilliant way of introducing his characters that, along with the names themselves, left a very distinct impression on the reader. The descriptions and the details found in usually no more than a paragraph of introduction was enough to leave no question what these people were really like. Take Mr. Bounderby, the blowhard banker in *Hard Times*:

He was a rich man: banker, merchant, manufacturer, and what not. A big, loud man, with a stare and a metallic laugh. A man made out of coarse material, which seemed to have been stretched to make so much of him. A man with a great puffed head and forehead, swelled veins in his temples, and such a strained skin to his face that it seemed to hold his eyes open and lift his eyebrows up. A man with a pervading appearance on him of being inflated like a balloon, ready to start.

Or the inimitable Veneerings from *Our Mutual Friend*, the ladder-climbing newly rich couple so careful to appear to be people of substance:

Mr. and Mrs. Veneering were bran-new people in a bran-new house in a bran-new quarter of London. Everything about the Veneerings was spick and span new. All their furniture was new, all their friends were new, all their servants were new, their plate was new, their carriage was new, their harness was new, their horses were new, their pictures were new, they themselves were new. . . . In the Veneering establishment, from the hall-chairs with the new coat of arms, to the grand pianoforte with the new action, and upstairs again to the new fire-escape, all things were in a state of high varnish and polish. And what was observable in the furniture, was observable in the Veneerings—the surface smelt a little too much of the workshop and was a trifle stickey.

for each person—either a physical detail, a behavior, or an aspect of their personality. Then give them a Dickensian moniker that matches. Your brother Mike is an athletic sports nut? Mikey Barbender! Uncle Hank is a butcher? He's Hamish Redbone. Your little sis is crazy about horses? She's Missy McBridle. Little cousin Abbie is a bit of a snitch? Abigail Tattleby!

What would Dickens have called his own son, Jack, who was known for his liveliness and practical jokes? Jack Sparks, or something mighty close. The inventive chef of a Dickens-style family might be known as Stewart Pepper. The family dentist? Dr. Crownacre.

Now turn it into a guessing game. Make a list of twenty people everyone in the family knows. Write each name on a slip of paper and put them in a hat. Each person chooses a name from the hat, creates a Dickensian name for the person, and the others have to guess who it really is.

Who's What?

Create a Dickensian name for a character with one of the following specific traits: sweet, talkative, sneaky, tongue-tied, gossipy, nosy, deceiving, merciful, arrogant, studious, hardworking, bragging, snobby, generous, flaky, anxious, or optimistic. What about someone who's a total slacker? Or very giggly? Or kind of pesky? Use a thesaurus and a baby name book to get ideas for pieces of the first and last names. Create a little cast of Dickens-worthy names and think of ways these characters might fit together in a story. Say Kath Chatterley is your talkative character. She is, improbably, the town librarian and is engaged to Scoop Mangleford, who's a reporter for a local newspaper famous for getting its stories all wrong. She lives next door to Ivy Pickets, the town wag, whose latest gossip threatens to turn the life of sweet kindergarten teacher Lilac Blooms upside down. Like that!

Sweet and Sour

Play a good guys/bad guys name game. This time, invent a name for a hero/heroine and a villain. Dream up fictional biographies of those people based on their names. Include mannerisms, appearance, and behavior. Make a list of the kinds of things these characters would say. Draw them in full costume. If your characters were in a movie, which actors would play them?

onomastics, n.: The study of the form and origin of family names.

Dickens Hall of Fame Names

Good Guys

Belle (*A Christmas Carol*)
The Cheeryble Brothers (*Nicholas Nickleby*)
Rosa Dartle (*David Copperfield*)
Amy Dorrit (*Little Dorrit*)
Sissy Jupe (*Hard Times*)
Rose Maylie (*Oliver Twist*)
Kit Nubbles (*Old Curiosity Shop*)
Clara Peggoty (*David Copperfield*)
Rosa (*Bleak House*)
Dora Spenlow (*David Copperfield*)
Nell Trent (*Old Curiosity Shop*)
Dolly Varden (*Barnaby Rudge*)

Bad Guys

Mrs. Badger (*Bleak House*)
Tite Barnacle (*Little Dorrit*)
Blathers (*Oliver Twist*)
Josiah Bounderby (*Hard Times*)
Sally Brass (*Old Curiosity Shop*)
Mr. Bumble (*Oliver Twist*)
Creakle (*David Copperfield*)
Thomas Gradgrind (*Hard Times*)
Mrs. MacStinger (*Dombey and Son*)
Mr. Pecksniff (*Martin Chuzzlewit*)
Peg Sliderskew (*Nicholas Nickleby*)
Mr. Snawley (*Nicholas Nickleby*)
Mr. Snagsby (*Bleak House*)
Hamilton and Anastasia Veneering (*Our Mutual Friend*)

Conversation Hearts

I'm transported back to the fourth grade every February when I get a confectionary whiff of Conversation Heart candies. "Be mine" "Hey Sugar" "True love"—what they lacked in punctuation, they more than made up for in good-hearted sweetness.

Valentine's Day is February 14.

What's the Palooza?

Overwhelm your family and friends with all kinds of Conversation Heart–style greetings. Do all your making and baking in the day or two before Valentine's Day.

Love Bundles

Drop a handful of Conversation Heart candies in the middle of six-by-six-inch squares of fabric. Tie each square into a little bundle with a length of ribbon and hang it on your family members' doorknobs as a treat to greet them first thing in the morning. Sneak them into your friends' lunch bags, lockers, or backpacks.

Conversation Cupcakes

Whip up a batch of cupcakes using your favorite flavor cake mix. Turn a store-bought container of white frosting into a bowl and mix in a few drops of red food coloring until it's a sweet pink. Write your own short Conversation Heart messages using gel-style decorator's frosting.

Make It Personal

Write a bunch of Conversation Heart messages specifically for a certain friend or member of your family. Think of details about their interests or hobbies for ideas. Do they have any quirks or distinguishing characteristics? For your blond mom? Yellow Lady. For your best friend who loves gymnastics? I Flip 4 U. For your frisky kitten? Krazy Kitty. Write these messages on your cupcakes. Or write them on a bunch of hearts cut out of construction paper and hide them in places you know each person will find them.

Who can play?
All ages.

What do we need?
Six-by-six-inch swatches of pretty fabric and eight-inch lengths of ribbon; a bag of Sweethearts Conversation Hearts. Muffin tin for cupcakes; your favorite flavor cake mix, white frosting, red food coloring; gel-type decorator's frosting in complementary colors; cupcake wrappers. White, red, and pink construction paper, scissors, and black markers. A book of love poems.

Running time?
A few hours altogether.

Budget?
$$

A Short, Sweet History of Conversation Hearts

Sweethearts Conversation Hearts have been rolling off the candy conveyor belt for more than a hundred years. First manufactured by the New England Confectionary Company (that's Necco, for short) in 1902, the candy hearts were an instant hit. Classic messages like "True Love" have stayed in the mix through the years, while others like "Dig It" and "Groovy" are retired to make room for more contemporary tidbits, like "Fax Me" or "Email Me." The Necco company manufactures close to 100,000 pounds of hearts a day, beginning right after Valentine's Day every year. If you're really head-over-heels for Conversation Hearts, you can have your own personalized message printed on a single batch of hearts. All you have to do is order a minimum of 3,500 pounds of hearts and you can have "Mom & Dad" hearts produced for their anniversary. That's a lot of sweet talk!

Sweet Somethings

Cut thirty or so small hearts out of construction paper. At breakfast on Valentine's Day, have everyone write one word on each heart. Try the words in different combinations to create an original Conversation Heart message. Or make a poem out of the words. Or have each person write a whole message on a heart and submit the best one to Necco, the company that makes Conversation Hearts. If it's good enough, Necco will include it in the following year's batch of Hearts. The only rule? Each saying can consist of no more than two lines of four letters each on the small hearts and two lines of six letters each on the large "motto" hearts. In other words, keep it short and sweet! Go to www.necco.com to submit your message.

Beatlemania

I don't know about you, but my favorite Beatle is John Lennon, hands down. With a little shrieking (but no fainting, please!), the Beatles are certainly something to whoop it up over.

What's the Palooza?

Plunge into the exuberance and undisputed musical genius of the Beatles and have a party no one will ever forget.

Dress Up

Invite friends to come dressed as any one of the Fab Four (Lennon or McCartney? Ringo or George? You know which one you are!) or in full Sgt. Pepper's Lonely Hearts Club Band regalia. Have a look at the trendsetting album cover on www.amazon.com and dress in a colorful coat or as any one of the characters in the montage. You can be Charlie Chaplin or Shirley Temple, a soccer player or a poet.

You can trace the evolution of the Beatles' music through their changing fashions over the years. Dress up as a Beatle from different eras; early mop tops and narrow suits and ties or collarless jackets, later

Who can play?

All ages love the theme; activities can be adapted to suit the age.

What do we need?

Beatles CDs and movies. Video camera, poster boards, drawing papers, bright colorful markers and/or poster paints (including neon colors if possible). And, depending on the activities you choose, karaoke machine or computer. Heavy construction paper and craft sticks for wig making. For costumes, store-bought or rented Beatles-style wigs, old clothes, props of all kinds for music video making. Plastic CD jewel boxes for designing CD covers.

Running time?

One to two hours, or more for Golden Slumbers sleepover.

Budget?

$$$

The Beatles appeared on the *Ed Sullivan Show* on February 19, 1964.

full-blown psychedelic trousers, even a flowing caftan straight from the ashram. Approximate Beatles style with a little help from Mom and Dad's closet, with permission. Or keep it simple and fringe an old pair of jeans and tie-dye a T-shirt.

Beatle-dos

Make Beatle-do masks out of construction paper. Style four distinct haircut patterns—don't forget the bangs!—out of sturdy brown or black construction paper. Cut out a bunch so guests can make a few masks and switch to "being" different Beatles. Attach a craft stick to the back of one side of the haircut mask with glue. Guests take the masks on and off as they slip into and out of character.

Album Art

Design your own album-cover art or rock poster. Display Beatles album covers on the wall or around the room. Make a poster listing of Beatles song titles and keep it in full view of guests. Everyone designs a new cover for a re-release of any of the Beatles albums; or choose from among the hundreds of Beatles song titles and illustrate it for a new album cover or a poster. Think of the glorious renditions guests might make of "Mean Mr. Mustard," "I Am the Walrus," "Piggies," "Octopus's Garden," "Good Day Sunshine," "Rocky Raccoon" or "Free as a Bird." Have extra poster boards and CD-cover-sized sheets of drawing paper available as the song titles inspire artists to make more than one piece of art. Guests may also want to invent their own record label, song title, and band and album names, and create an original CD cover or poster for the work.

Beatles Song Sampler

"All My Loving"
"Can't Buy Me Love"
"Carry That Weight"
"Dig a Pony"
"Don't Let Me Down"
"Do You Want to Know a Secret"
"Eight Days a Week"
"Fixing a Hole"
"Free as a Bird"
"Golden Slumbers"
"Got to Get You into My Life"
"A Hard Day's Night"
"Here Comes the Sun"
"Her Majesty"
"Hey Jude"
"The Hippy Hippy Shake"
"I Am the Walrus"
"I'm Happy Just to Dance with You"
"I Saw Her Standing There"
"Lady Madonna"
"Lend Me Your Comb"
"Long Tall Sally"
"Lovely Rita"

"March of the Meanies"
"Maxwell's Silver Hammer"
"Mean Mr. Mustard"
"Michelle"
"Mr. Moonlight"
"Ob-La-di, Ob-La-Da"
"Octopus's Garden"
"Paperback Writer"
"Penny Lane"
"Piggies"
"Please Mr. Postman"
"Rocky Raccoon"
"Savoy Truffle"
"Sgt. Pepper's Lonely Heart's Club Band"
"The Sheik of Araby"
"Strawberry Fields Forever"
"Taxman"
"Ticket to Ride"
"When I'm Sixty-Four"
"With a Little Help from My Friends"
"Yesterday"
"You Really Got a Hold on Me"
"Your Mother Should Know"

Make Like MTV, Mate

Create your own Beatles music videos. Groups of four choose a Beatles song and choreograph a music video to be filmed and played back at the end of the party. Wear wigs or Beatles haircut masks and put together silly costumes for play-acting Beatles' tunes. Have ideas and suggestions at the ready. Young guests might opt for "Yellow Submarine," "Love Me Do," or "When I'm Sixty-Four." Older fans may want "Maxwell's Silver Hammer," "Her Majesty," or "A Hard Day's Night." All ages can sing and dance in costume to most any Beatles song and have a blast videotaping the performance for replay at the end of the party.

Just Sing It

Your stereo blasts Beatles tunes throughout this party, but a highlight might be organized Beatles singalongs or Beatles karaoke, where groups of four choose a Beatles song and perform it for the group—preferably with masks! Beatles karaoke CDs are available from Amazon.com, or go to any one of the Beatles karaoke Web sites to download MIDI files of Beatles tunes. Karaoke machines are readily available for rent in music or electronics stores. You can also display Beatles lyrics on your computer screen and sing along with MIDI files. Videotape the performances, of course.

I'm Happy Just to Dance with You

Guests make up dance moves to Beatles songs and dance them with abandon. The "Twist and Shout," the "March of the Meanies," "Dizzy Miss Lizzy," or the "Hippy Hippy Shake." Teach everyone the moves; put on any one of the songs and have a leader call out which dance to do. This might become a recurring theme of the party. Whenever the leader calls out "Hippy Hippy Shake," or better yet, when the designated DJ puts on the song, everyone stops what they're doing to do the corresponding dance.

Why Does a Beatle Cross the Road?

The Beatles' *Abbey Road* album cover sparked rampant controversy over its possible meanings. Why were the handsome Beatles, suited up and confidently striding forward, crossing the proverbial road? Why was Paul McCartney barefoot? Have guests go outside in groups of four, crossing the road (with parental supervision, and carefully, of course!) in positions similar to the Beatles. Use a digital or Polaroid camera to take pictures of guests posturing as the Fab Four. Use the pictures to design a CD cover.

Nonsense

Make a complete list of Beatles song titles available for everyone to read on a poster board. Guests try to put three or four song titles together to make a story. Play charades using the names of Beatles tunes. No humming is allowed during charades, of course. Ask guests to come up with a guess as to the true meaning of *Abbey Road.* Place written guesses in a Beatles wig, read them aloud, and have everyone guess who wrote which response.

Golden Slumbers

Turn your Beatlemania party into a sleepover party. Wind down after making music videos by watching Beatles movies on DVD or video. Choose among *A Hard Day's Night, Help! Yellow Submarine, Let It Be,* and *Magical Mystery Tour,* or rent them all for a Golden Slumbers marathon.

They look like shaggy Peter Pans with their mushroom haircuts and high white shirt collars. The precise nature of their charm remains mysterious.

—*Time* magazine, November 1963

Leap!

If ever there was a day that begged to be seized, it's February 29. Since it only comes every four years, fill it with extraordinary activities—turn cartwheels, learn to juggle, leap and lunge like a pirate à la Gilbert and Sullivan's *Pirates of Penzance.*

What's the Palooza?

Stage a snip of William S. Gilbert and Sir Arthur Sullivan's *Pirates of Penzance* and then party like a pirate! The main plot of this swashbuckling comic operetta hinges on the fact that the orphaned hero, Frederic, was born on February 29, or Leap Year Day. Just when Frederic expects liberation from a gang of singing, dancing pirates on his twenty-first birthday, he realizes the dire consequences of his Leap Year birth: he is not twenty turning twenty-one, but five turning six. As a result, he's bound to the pirates for the next sixty

The Lowdown on Leap Year

In 1582, the bosses in charge of time and calendars decided to add one day to the annual calendar every four years. Here's why: A year is actually a tad longer than 365 days; it takes more like 365 and a quarter days for the earth to make one orbit around the sun, which is what we refer to as a year. The calendar bosses were worried that if they didn't take corrective measures, the quarter days would begin to add up, and eventually the calendar would begin to get ahead of the seasons. So they added a day (February 29) every four years to bring the calendar back in line with the earth's motion around the sun.

Make It a Party!

Invites: A battered bit of brown bag or tea-stained paper written and decorated like a pirate's map. Use as many pirate words as you can think of, matey! Go to www.talklikeapirate.com for loads of inspiration.

Food and Decor: Invite guests to dress up as pirates or damsels or major-generals. Decorate liberally with pirate doodads, from skull-and-crossbones flags to gold doubloons (chocolate, of course) in a chest. Go to www.deadmentellnotales.com to visit Billy Bones's Pirate Locker for ideas and cool pirately items to order for your party. Serve biscuits and crackers, chili, jerk chicken or baby shrimp, fruit salad, and limeade.

Activities: Invite guests to come prepared to perform their own bit of *Pirates,* either a song or fun bit of dialogue. Take photos of performances. Make Leap Year resolutions—things you vow to do when you "find some extra time" (like Leap Year Day!).

Favors: Eye patches, bandannas, gold candy coins, bags of Pirate Booty.

Who can play?
Ages 6 and up.

What do we need?
Pirates of Penzance video and audio recording; thrift store/dress-up clothes and accessories (eye patches, head scarves, plastic or cardboard swords, and so on) to create pirate costumes and/or major-general costume; large appliance boxes, duct tape, paint, large dowel or broomstick, old pillowcase, small step stool; pirate snacks (as below).

Running time?
Several hours to create cardboard pirate ship set, assemble costumes, and learn the words to a *Pirates* song. Less than an hour for your performance and party.

Budget?
$$

years. And this little brain twister is only one of the plots of this rollicking story!

Prepare for your big leap by renting *Pirates of Penzance* at the video store. The stars, including Kevin Kline, Linda Ronstadt, and Angela Lansbury, have great fun with the rousing pirate songs, acrobatics, tap dancing, and overall comic merriment. Watching this performance a couple of times will give you a good idea of the story line, as well as the nature of the different characters. Study the lively, athletic Pirate King (Kline), the earnest and amusing Frederic (Rex Smith), the sweet and demure Mabel (Ronstadt), the ditzy maid, Ruth (Lansbury), and especially the riotously funny Major-General Stanley (George Rose).

Choose a song and/or a short scene to stage for your family. "I Am the Very Model of a Modern Major-General" is a likely candidate; it's probably the most famous patter song ever written and a blast to learn to

Leap Year Day occurs on February 29.

patter song, n. phrase: A comic song in opera or operetta, characterized by a quick tempo and rhythmic patterns in the lyrics, which often also contain tongue-twisting phrases.

sing. Or put together a band of pirates and sing "A Rollicking Band of Pirates We." Or combine Frederic, Mabel, and "the Girls" to sing a colorful "How Beautifully Blue the Sky." Listen to a CD several times to help you learn your song and get the spirit of it running through your head.

Forage in your closets and at thrift stores for components of your costumes. Make a ship's forecastle (f'c'sle in pirate talk!) out of cardboard appliance boxes as a mini-set for a pirate song. Fly a pirate flag from a broomstick. Arrange coolers (treasure chests!) and overturned buckets (grog barrels!) for props. Rehearse your performance a few times. Set up a carpenter's work light as a spotlight on your stage. At showtime, turn down the house lights and give it all you've got!

Pirate Snacks

When they weren't swilling tankards of ale, pirates liked to snack on a few delicacies such as:

hardtack: A dried, tooth-crackable bread.

terrapin: Turtle meat.

lobscouse: A meat-and-dried-biscuit stew.

salted meats and fish: Salt preserved the meat and fish (and helped to disguise its often nasty taste).

limes: Vitamin C–rich citrus fruit that helped prevent scurvy. Argh.

march
paloozas

Seasons & Senses

American naturalist John Burroughs once said, "I go to nature to be soothed and healed, and to have my senses put in order." Even in the dead of winter, you can visit a botanical garden or arboretum and get a healthy dose of the glow of growing things to make you stretch and yearn for spring to spring to life. Or you can wait for nature to do her thing the same way you wait for the bus—it comes, eventually it always comes.

Who can play?
Ages 9–12.

What do we need?
Notebook or sketchpad, colored pencils, markers or watercolor paints and brush; tape recorder and field guide to birds; vegetable or flower seeds, potting soil, and ceramic or plastic pots.

Running time?
An afternoon in the earliest moments of spring, and all throughout the seasons.

Budget?
$$

What's the Palooza?

"Springtime is upon us" is the opening phrase of the sonnet that precedes one of the most famous and frequently played pieces of classical music, Antonio Vivaldi's *The Four Seasons*. Vivaldi's composition is made up of a cycle of concertos in the Baroque style that evoke and mimic both the subtle and startling changes of the year's seasons. "La Primavera"—springtime—is just when you should start to engage your five senses with the four seasons and plunge into the wonders of nature.

Spring Sleuth

Begin with your eyes. Starting in late February and early March, scope out your own yard, your neighbors' yards, your park and schoolyard. Tuck a notebook under your arm and pretend you're a detective, looking for clues that spring is on the way. If you live in a colder climate, first you might find witch hazel, a flowering shrub that blooms yellow or red in the very last days of winter when everything else is still asleep; this may be a first hint that spring is on the way. Next you might spy snowdrops, crocuses, and hellebores peeping through snow. Soon after you may spot primrose, sweet violet, bleeding heart, or tender daffodils making their early appearance. The best part of this little dance of spring is seeing the entire cast of bloomers take turns coming on the stage. Take note of the plants you see coming to life and the order in which they appear. Use a good seasonal plant guide to help you identify them. Make sketches of your favorites. Or make a treasure map of your yard, marking the spots where evidence of spring first appears with little drawings of the plants you discover. As you

Flower Power

Make your own flower sachets or potpourri to bring the scent of spring or summer into your sock drawer next winter. Collect scented flowers throughout the season and hang them in bunches from a string to dry. They should be in a dry spot in your home that doesn't get too much sunlight. When they're good and dry—this could take a month or more—remove the petals of the flowers and lightly crush them into a bowl. Roses, carnations, hibiscus, lavender, and violets are especially fragrant, and sage, rosemary, and thyme are herbs that work well, too. Combine your ingredients and scatter drops of essential oil (you can get this at a good crafts store) over the mixture using an eyedropper. Stir, and place the mixture in a brown paper bag lined with wax paper. Seal the bag and leave in a dry, cool place for two weeks, stirring the contents every other day. When it's ready, scoop the mixture into cotton hankies, tie them with pretty ribbon, and drop them in drawers or hang them in closets all over the house.

Composer Antonio Vivaldi was born on March 4, 1678.

move through later spring, summer, and fall, you can create new maps that show the plants that appear over time. Where the first crocus once poked through the half-frozen soil, eventually a succession of spring and summertime plants and flowers will be giving their vigorous performances.

Making Scents of Things

Scientists estimate that humans can distinguish about 10,000 smells. Our sense of smell is one of our two chemical senses (the other is taste), which means we get sensory information through the chemicals that are released into the air—everything from the whiff of a gardenia bloom to a smoky fire to a fishy fish. Take an olfactory expedition, a tramp around your yard or park

Make It a Party!

Invites: Flower-shaped invites, perhaps spritzed with a floral dash of scent. "Come to a garden party—and don't forget your green thumb!"

Food and Decor: If it's an indoor party, set up the room like a garden, with backyard folding chairs and potted plants all around. To grow instant grass, throw a green blanket on the floor. Play Vivaldi's *The Four Seasons,* of course. Serve dainty cucumber sandwiches, ants on a log (celery sticks filled with cream cheese and topped with raisins), lemonade, lettuce-wrapped spring rolls, a fruit salad with kiwis, honeydew melon, and green grapes, and cupcakes decorated with a variety of frosting flowers.

Activities: A flowerpot-painting extravaganza, using simple clay pots and ceramic paints or markers. After pots are dolled up, fill with commercial potting soil and plant quick-and-easy-germinating seeds like wheatgrass. Or make wind chimes to turn your front porch into a tinkly concert hall. Get sets of metal kitchen measuring cups or spoons and wire whisks at the dollar store. Decorate the measuring cups (or spoons) with flower, bug, and bird decals or waterproof paint. Attach each cup to a different rung of the whisk with slightly different lengths of sturdy string. Hang your creation in a spot where it will catch a breeze and make music.

Favors: Miniature clay pots, packets of seeds, small plastic bags of potting soil, and gummy worms.

with a nose for the different smells you can identify. Did you catch the fresh scent of a pine tree? Doesn't it even *smell* green? What does the air smell like after a good rain? Have you ever had a sniff of skunk cabbage? Take a late-spring field trip to a nursery or botanical garden and head for the lavender, azaleas, honeysuckle, and summer jasmine. These are very distinctive scents, lush and memorable. Can you smell the difference between one variety of lavender and another? You've got a good sniffer! For a real challenge, see if you can hunt down a whiff of a Japanese apricot tree, a Mexican orange shrub, or a lemon daylily. Become a scent connoisseur, a seasoned collector of exotic smells.

Make a list of all the smells you associate with the seasons where you live, from the smell of a dry, cold day before it snows to the smell of a freshly cut lawn.

The Four Seasons

Antonio Vivaldi's *Le Quattro Stagioni,* or *The Four Seasons,* has been performed by some of the finest orchestras and instrumental soloists in the world, partly because it's such a signature piece of classical music and partly because it's so much fun to do. The first recording was made in 1942; there are now over 120 different recordings currently available, and *The Four Seasons* has surpassed Beethoven's Fifth as the most popular of all classical works. Vivaldi lovers live to argue over what's the best, most definitive performance, but we won't jump into that fray. Here are a few CDs that will not disappoint:

Le Quattro Stagioni, composed by Antonio Vivaldi, conducted by Trevor Pinnock, performed by the English Concert, with featured violinist Simon Standage (Archiv Produktion, 1990).

The Four Seasons, composed by Antonio Vivaldi, performed by the English Chamber Orchestra and Nigel Kennedy (EMI, 1989).

The Four Seasons, composed by Antonio Vivaldi, conducted by Leonard Bernstein, performed in 1964 by the New York Philharmonic with John Corigliano (Sony, 1998).

The Four Seasons, composed by Antonio Vivaldi, conducted by Bernardino Molinari, and performed by the Santa Cecilia Academy of Rome, was the first recording of *The Four Seasons,* made in 1942 (Aura Classics, reissued 2003).

Also have a taste of William Christie's Les Artes Florissants, who are doing so much to revive the appreciation for Baroque music. Try *Les Lumières du Baroque: Une Encyclopédie Musicale.*

baroque, adj.: A style of musical composition that thrived in Europe from about 1600 to 1750, known for its elaborate ornamentation, dramatic arcs, and an overall balance of different parts.

What do you think "the smell of fall in the air" is? Leaves? Apples? School?!? Some of these smells are what make up your smell memory, which is very sharp and lasts a lifetime. Someday, when you're old, you'll catch a sniff of one of these familiar smells and be snapped right back to your childhood.

Sounds of Summer

Summer brings "the cuckoo's voice . . . then sweet songs of the turtle dove," wrote Vivaldi. The bird sounds in the air are an important part of the seasonal picture of where you live. What are the first birds you see and hear in springtime? Do you know the names of the noisy ones making a racket outside your window on a summer morning? Have you ever heard an owl hoot or a hawk squawk? Be a field reporter and tape-record the bird sounds particular to where you live—the mourning doves or pigeons cooing, the woodpecker hammering on a tree, the caw-caws bossing each other around. Use a good field guide to birds, such as one of the Peterson's guides, to try to identify your birds by sight and sound. Author Roger Tory Peterson was a master at verbal descriptions of the appearance and sounds of birds. Tape other seasonal sounds (as are depicted in *The Four Seasons*) such as barking dogs, flowing water, thunder, rustling leaves. Create an audio Encyclopedia of Seasonal Sounds near your home!

Haste Makes Taste

Vivaldi saw autumn as a time to "celebrate with song and dance the harvest." Maybe the best way to investigate the marvel of Mother Nature is to harvest your own crop of earthly goodies. One of the easiest vegetables to grow is the radish, and you don't have to wait forever to reap the fruits of your labor; you can grow a radish in about a month. Fill a six-inch clay or plastic pot with potting soil and plant radish seeds according to seed packet directions. Be sure to offer your seedling plenty of sunlight and don't let the soil dry out. Radishes are pretty, but kind of spicy tasting all by themselves. Think about growing a whole salad—lettuce, carrot, onion—to serve up with your radish. Or try growing some wild and crazy edible plants like alfalfa, fennel, and chervil. There are also edible flowers you can grow, too, including calendula, English daisies, nasturtium, and pansies. Be careful—once your thumb goes green, it never goes back.

Good Books

Grow Your Own Pizza: Gardening Plans and Recipes for Kids, by Constance Hardesty and Jeff McClung

Dig, Plant, Grow: A Kid's Guide to Gardening, by Felder Rushing

Roots, Shoots, Buckets & Boots, by Sharon Lovejoy

Plants for Every Season, by the American Horticultural Society

Peterson's First Guide to North American Birds, by Roger Tory Peterson

Mush!

Rugged mountain passes. Arctic chill. Moose herds. While an elite few get to experience the actual thrill of the Iditarod, anyone can root for a musher and get a taste of the ultimate in Alaskan adventure.

What's the Palooza?

For the past thirty years, thousands of eager sled dogs, mostly Alaskan huskies, have made the thousand-plus-mile trek north from downtown Anchorage to Nome, Alaska, in one of the most demanding sporting events of all time, the Iditarod. Designed to celebrate the history and tradition of dogsledding in Alaska, and inspired by an actual event from 1925 when dogsledders relayed diphtheria medication to the town of Nome in the middle of a devastating outbreak, the Iditarod race today is as arduous and challenging as ever. And while mushers—the dogsled riders—glory in the spectacular setting and the physical demands of the race, most claim the bond they form with their team of huskies to be the most gratifying feature of the Iditarod.

Team Spirit

How to get in on the fun? Adopt a musher and his team and cheer them on to the finish line in Alaska's Iditarod Trail Sled Dog Race, "the last great race on earth." Find a list of musher names on any of several Iditarod Web sites. The official site is www.iditarod.com. If you begin this palooza on the ceremonial Saturday start date for the Iditarod, which is always in Anchorage, Alaska, on the first Saturday in March, take a little time in advance

Red Lanterns and Widow's Lamps

In the days when dogsleds were used to carry mail and freight, kerosene lamps were lit at roadhouses to light the way for dogsleds known to be on the trail. Lamps were not extinguished until mushers reached their destinations. Today a "widow's lamp" is always lit at the finish line of the Iditarod and stays lit until the last musher finishes the race.

The last musher to finish the Iditarod is awarded a red lantern, a practice that began as a joke to suggest that the musher needed a light to find his way because he was so far away from the others. But the red lantern has also become a symbol of never giving up on the race.

Musher, n.: From the French *marche,* meaning "to march." Originates from the Gold Rush days when anyone who traveled in the northwest was called a "musher," whether they traveled by dogsled or not. Also refers to anyone who travels by dog team on a dogsled.

to read bios of several mushers, past winners and rookies alike, and choose the one you'd like to cheer on. Each musher is given an actual starting time for Sunday (called the "Restart"), which happens twenty miles north of Anchorage in Wasilla.

Once you have your musher's starting time, make a timeline of checkpoints along the trail on a large poster board. The northern and southern Iditarod routes alternate each year (the northern route is run in even years, the southern route in odd years), but each begins with the "Restart" in Wasilla and ends in Nome, so record your "Restart" time and date at Wasilla.

The Iditarod begins on the first Saturday of March.

Anchorage
Eagle River
Wasilla
Knik Lake
Yentna
Skwentna
Finger Lake
Rainy Pass
Rohn
Nikolai
McGrath
Takotna
Ophir
Cripple
Ruby
Galena
Nulato
Kaltag
Unalakleet
Shaktoolik
Koyuk
Elim
Golovin
White Mountain
Safety
Nome

Mark and label your checkpoints on the poster board. Make note of your musher's Restart date and time on your timeline at Wasilla. When the race begins, go to www.iditarod.com for updates and news of your musher's progress and checkpoint arrivals; mark them dutifully on your timeline. Get family members to adopt mushers, too; check your musher's progress together online.

Print pictures of your musher and dogsled team from the Internet and decorate your timeline. Look for maps and other Iditarod-related images and make a collage around the timeline: huskies, dogsleds, Alaskan scenery, bears, moose, dog booties and jackets. If your musher has commercial sponsors, print out sponsor logos and include them in the collage.

Most mushers love to receive mail from Iditarod fans. Look for the snail mail or e-mail address on any of the popular Iditarod sites for your musher and send a letter of support. See especially www.iditarod.com, www.cabelasiditarod.com, or www.dogsled.com for news and information on how to contact mushers.

Fantasy Mush

Pretend you are racing the Iditarod and make up a fantasy dogsled team. Choose them from the dogs that are actually running the race and are profiled on Iditarod sites. Or make up your own ultra-fantasy dogs—hey, they don't even have to be huskies! On your fantasy team, Pinky the Poodle could be the best lead dog that ever ran the race! Iditarod rules require a minimum of twelve dogs to start the race, and a maximum of sixteen. What are your dogs' personalities and names? Have they raced before? What do they like to eat? Research what real sled dogs eat at www.iditarod.com. Assign your dogs places in your "towline," the special hitch used to pull the sled. *Lead dogs* like to run in front and listen best to musher commands. *Swing dogs* help set the pace and turn the team. *Team dogs* follow the tails in front of them and provide the constant pull. *Wheel dogs* help to steer the sled. Remember to vary dog positions like the real mushers do.

Iditarod Lit

Get into the mood by digging into some great books about the Iditarod. Gary Paulsen is perhaps the best-known children's author to have covered Iditarod territory, both literally (he was a musher in 1983) and figuratively (he's written a number of Iditarod and dogsled-themed books). *Winterdance* is his gripping nonfiction account of his running the Iditarod race. *Woodsong* is his autobiographical relating of his life-long love of dog-sledding. *Dogsong* is Paulsen's novel

Make It a Party!

Invites: Print the Iditarod route map from the Internet and invite guests to the "last great race on earth." Write "1,049 Miles" on the front of your invitation. Explain on the inside that the Iditarod race is roughly 1,049 miles—at least 1,000 miles plus 49 for the forty-ninth state. Or decorate invitations with pictures of Alaskan huskies.

Food and Decor: Hang maps of Alaska on the walls and use them as tablecloths. Highlight the Iditarod course on each map. Drape white sheets over all the furniture in the room—that's the snow! Make dinner a "Mushers Banquet" of mushroom barley soup, iceberg lettuce salad, and chocolate "moose" cake. Or make your own Iditarod ice cream sundaes.

Activities: Adopt mushers, of course, and make up fantasy teams. Write a letter to your musher. Make team banners or dog booties out of felt. While you're at it, make a musher's hat out of felt. Decorate it with crazy, wintery bric-a-brac. Make custom trail mix with favorite ingredients and package in specially designed and decorated brown paper lunch bags. Watch a video of *Balto* or *Snow Dogs*. Even better, go to www.dogsled.com/av to watch streaming video of the race as it's happening.

Favors: Trail mix. Snow globe. Paperback copy of Gary Paulsen's *Winterdance*.

Southern Route Checkpoints

Anchorage
Eagle River
Wasilla
Knik
Yentna
Skwentna
Finger Lake
Rainy Pass
Rohn
Nikolai
McGrath
Takotna
Ophir
Iditarod
Shageluk
Anvik
Grayling
Eagle Island
Kaltag
Unalakleet
Shaktoolik
Koyuk
Elim
Golovin
White Mountain
Safety
Nome

Hike up: Used to start up the team; also means "Go faster." Note: "Mush" is not really used as the start command. Sometimes mushers do start with "Okay, let's go!" or "All right!"

Whoa! Means stop. Teams rarely obey this command on its own; usually, the brakes have to be used to get the dogs to stop.

Gee: Move right.

Haw: Move left.

Straight ahead: Use at intersections or when passing other teams or snowmobiles.

Easy: Slow down.

No! Means just what it says. May imply *yes* to most sled dogs.

about a fourteen-year-old Eskimo boy's dog-sledding journey to find himself. Read about alpha males in the Jack London classics, *White Fang* or *Call of the Wild*. Read Scott O'Dell's Iditarod novel, *Black Star, Bright Dawn* and Seymour Reit's *Race Against Death: True Story about the Far North,* the story of Togo and Balto, the true-life heros of the lifesaving race to save Nome's children in 1925. Younger readers can check out *Akiak* by Robert J. Blake or *Where's the Boss?* by Lois Harter.

March Hare

It's March! What better excuse do you need to revisit Lewis Carroll's *Alice's Adventures in Wonderland*? This palooza tips its mad hat to the March Hare and a harebrained scheme for making up riddles.

What's the Palooza?

Lewis Carroll was mad for riddles and word games, and he used them as often as he could in his writing. Read "A Mad Tea-Party," chapter 7 from *Alice's Adventures in Wonderland,* aloud at breakfast, then spend the better part of your day making up rhyming riddles and sharing them with (or foisting them off on?) your friends.

A riddle is a puzzle in the form of a question or rhyme that contains clues to its answer. One easy way to start a riddle is to choose a word from a topic you are interested in and make up an alphabet riddle for it. As an example, since this is a book about celebrations, we will make up a riddle for which the answer is "party." For the first clue, use the beginning and ending letters of the word "party." So the riddle may begin:

I start with p and end with y.

Then, to create your rhyming clue, make a list of words that rhyme with *y:*

Fly	My
By	Lie
Why	Pie
Sky	Try

Who can play?
Ages 6–9.

What do we need?
A copy of *Alice's Adventures in Wonderland*. Pencil and paper or a small journal. Rhyming dictionary is optional.

Running time?
Give yourself an hour, but making riddles could turn into a lifelong hobby.

Budget?
Absolutely free.

mad as a march hare, adj. phrase: A touch crazy and unpredictable. It is said to refer to the way rabbits get a little wild-eyed in the early spring when their mating season gets under way.

Which of these words inspires your final clue? How about:

I start with p and end with y,
On your next birthday, give me a try.

List interesting words you want to make riddles about. Think of favorite pastimes, sports, foods, school subjects. List unusual or favorite words. Or make riddles from words found in "A Mad Tea-Party": clock, pocket, asleep, time, tea, butter, milk jug, and so forth. When you get the hang of writing riddles, expand them to include more than a couple of sentences and clues.

When you've made up lots of riddles, copy them over in your best handwriting and make a book out of them. Fasten loose-leaf pages together in a booklet or use a small notebook or journal. Illustrate your riddle book and share it with friends and family.

Riddl-iculous

As imagined in Carroll's "A Mad Tea-Party," the joke's on Alice that there is no answer to the Mad Hatter's riddle: "Why is a raven like a writing desk?" Using the same question format as Carroll, make up your own ridiculous riddles. Think of highly unusual combinations. Why is a stereo like a banana? Why is a fruitcake like a gas station? Your riddles may or may not have answers. You decide!

Mad Caps and More

The Dormouse tells a convoluted story at the Mad Hatter's tea party, in which three sisters are at first learning to draw treacle out of a well (this, of course, makes no sense to Alice), but then the Dormouse says they are learning to draw "all manner of things—everything that begins with an M . . . such as mouse-traps,

Why Is a Riddle Like a Writing Desk?

Lewis Carroll was asked so often about the Mad Hatter's riddle that he actually included the following preface to the 1896 edition of *Alice's Adventures in Wonderland*: "Enquiries have been so often addressed to me, as to whether any answer to the Hatter's Riddle can be imagined, that I may as well put on record here what seems to me to be a fairly appropriate answer, viz: 'Because it can produce a few notes, tho they are *very* flat; and it is never put with the wrong end in front!' "

This after-the-fact explanation only partly made sense to those vexed by the riddle; there was something unclear about the last bit. That's because as Carroll originally wrote his explanation, it read: "and it is *nevar* put with the wrong end in front!" Unfortunately, an overeager editor of the American edition had "corrected" the spelling of the word *nevar*, which, of course, is *raven* spelled backward and critical to his answer to the riddle.

and the moon, and memory, and muchness." Take a cue from the story and draw a quirky, Wonderlandish collection of things that begin with *M.* Be sure to try your hand at drawing "muchness"!

Make It a Doublet

Lewis Carroll invented a word game called Doublets, which has become popularly known over the years as Word Ladders, Word Chains, or Laddergrams, among other variations. This simple (but tricky!) game takes one word and asks you to turn it into another through a series of letter changes, anywhere from three linking words up to seven. So the Doublet called PUT MILK INTO PAIL wants you to get from the word *milk* to the word *pail* using three linking words. How about *milk* to *mill* to *pill* to *pall* to *pail?* Can you TURN OIL INTO GAS in four links? Try *oil* to *nil* to *nip* to *nap* to *gap* to *gas.* Create your own

"Have you guessed the riddle yet?" the Hatter said, turning to Alice again.

"No, I give it up," Alice replied: "what's the answer?"

"I haven't the slightest idea," said the Hatter.

"Nor I," said the March Hare.

Alice sighed wearily. "I think you might do something better with the time," she said, "than waste it in asking riddles that have no answers."

—"A Mad Tea-Party," in
*Alice's Adventures in
Wonderland*

Good Books

Check out *The Annotated Alice,* which includes the original text and many illustrations from *Alice's Adventures in Wonderland* and *Through the Looking Glass and What Alice Found There* by Lewis Carroll, as well as juicy, newsy notes alongside the text by Martin Gardner. You really feel you know *Alice* inside and out when you read this book. Also look for Martin Gardner's *Universe in a Handkerchief: Lewis Carroll's Mathematical Recreations, Games, Puzzles and Word Plays,* a fun look at all of Carroll's fascinations with words, math, and logic.

Make It a Party!

Invites: Use our party riddle above on your invitation to invite guests to a March Hare/Mad Hatter Riddle Writing Party.

Food and Decor: A large table set for traditional tea, and with extra place settings! An oversize watch made out of poster board that tells what year it is, but not the o'clock. Serve bread and butter, scones, crumpets, tiny watercress sandwiches on white bread with no crusts, strawberries and cream, and fruity herbal teas.

Activities: Decorate small journals for riddle writing. Play Hounds and Hares, an old outdoor game in which the hares drop pieces of paper along a trail and the hounds, following the "scent" of paper, try to catch them. Do a dramatic reading from Carroll's "A Mad Tea-Party" or stage a puppet show of the scene with homemade felt or sock puppets.

Favors: Riddle journals, a paperback copy of *Alice.*

Doublets starting with a short simple word that you fool around with transforming into a cleverly related word, as with *milk* and *pail* and *oil* and *gas.* Look for words in the tea-party chapter to play Doublets with.

Sidewalk Café

Le Tour Eiffel, the world-famous emblem of the City of Lights, is of course best viewed while having a crusty roll and a cup of pure arabica at one of the many sidewalk cafés in Paris. This palooza stirs up a bit of café society right in your own home.

What's the Palooza?

Paris's historic café culture is romanticized for good reason. Cafés have been the hub of social life for centuries; Hemingway and Picasso hung out at Les Deux Magots while the existentialists favored Café de Flore a few doors down on the boulevard Saint-Germain-des-Prés. The oldest café in Paris, Le Procope, is known to have been a happening spot for Voltaire, Rousseau, and Benjamin Franklin. While away an hour or two at your own French café. Set up an at-home café, indoors or outside on your patio or driveway. You be the maître d' or patron or both; sit alone with a book or chatting with a friend. Discuss endlessly important matters of the day such as art, politics, music—or speak of nothing at all. Be a *flaneur* (connoisseur of street life) as you watch the passersby. Have a bite to eat and enjoy the scenery. Is that Ernest Hemingway writing something on a napkin over there? Why, no, but I'm certain I do see Picasso sketching on a tablecloth in the back.

Le Café Chez Vous

Prepare to open Le Café Chez Vous—the Café at Your House. Decorate with posters of the Eiffel Tower, Sacré Coeur, Arc de Triomph, or other Paris landmarks. Cover

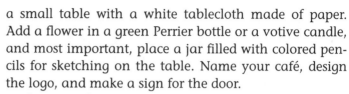

a small table with a white tablecloth made of paper. Add a flower in a green Perrier bottle or a votive candle, and most important, place a jar filled with colored pencils for sketching on the table. Name your café, design the logo, and make a sign for the door.

Play French music to add to the mood. Mix traditional French songs and contemporary French pop. The recordings of Edith Piaf are perfect: "Non, Je Ne Regrette Rien" or "La Vie, L'Amour." Ah, *oui.*

Dress the Part

The French are famous for their pulled-together, crisp style. Tie a scarf elegantly around your neck and add some red lipstick. *Voilà! Je ne sais quoi!* Wear a beret and striped sailor shirt for a classic look, or wear any combination of red, white, and blue, the colors of the French Revolution (and favorite colors of our own!). The red represents courage, the white purity, and the blue freedom. The French dress simply, but with every detail just so. Wear khakis and collared shirt, but with the cuffs casually (but stylishly) rolled, of course.

Mangez-vous!

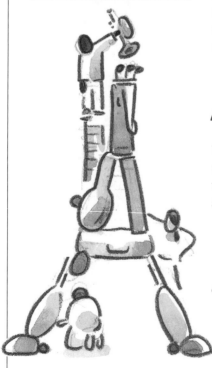

While the French love a fancy meal, food in the cafés is usually as simple (and delicious) as ham on a baguette with good mustard. Serve pastry, croissants, tomato slices, quiche, sliced meats and cheese, fruits, and crackers. No sidewalk café is complete without good coffee. If the patron(s) of your café don't drink coffee, serve an authentic *chocolat chaud* (hot chocolate) sprinkled with nutmeg. Or make it a cappuccino, hold-the-espresso: steam a cup of milk until it's frothy and sprinkle with a bit of cocoa powder. Coffee service at Café de Flore, one of the most famous cafés in all of Paris, comes on a small silver tray, in a white cup and saucer, with a sugar packet, bitter chocolate wrapped in foil, and a glass of water. Root around in the cupboard for nice cups and serving pieces (use with permission, natch) for a tasteful presentation. Create a chalkboard menu for your café.

The Eiffel Tower in Paris first opened for visitors on March 31, 1889.

Artiste, Artiste

Sketch the Eiffel Tower on the white tablecloth using colored pencils. (Georges Seurrat, Pierre Bonnard, Raoul Dufy, and Marc Chagall are among the many artists to have rendered the Eiffel Tower over the years.) Or write a poem, song lyric, or story that somehow makes use of the monument. Sketch your friend's portrait. Or the Paris street scene. Many artists found inspiration in the sidewalk cafés of Paris, and you can, too!

People Watching

Raid magazines for pictures of interesting people and make a collage of them. Pretend these are the people you see walking by your café and invent their stories. A

The Tower Itself

The Eiffel Tower was designed by Gustave Eiffel and constructed for the Paris Exposition Universelle (world's fair) in 1889. It is 984 feet high and is made of an iron frame, supported on four piers, from which four columns rise to meet each other and form one shaft. The tower was the tallest structure in the world until the Chrysler Building in New York was built in 1930. The Eiffel Tower is painted every seven years in three shades of "Tour Eiffel brown," with the lightest shade at the top and the darkest at the bottom. In the twenty-three months it took to build, a fury of criticism and protest from the highbrow Parisian art world swirled about the project. Their objections melted away when the world fell instantly in love with the structure, prompting two million people to visit in its inaugural year, with more than six million visiting annually today. Go to www.tour-eiffel.fr/teiffel/uk/ for loads of fabulous facts and figures about the tower, as well as a virtual tour and aerial view from the tower itself.

man walks by, holding a bouquet of flowers: who are they for? Where is that woman in the red dress going? To meet the man in the bowler hat?

Escargot

Play an old authentic French sidewalk game that's like hopscotch called *Escargot* (the French word for "snail"). Draw a six- to eight-foot-wide snail (spiral) shape on the sidewalk with chalk, then divide the snail into fifteen boxes. The first player must hop on one foot from box to box all the way to the center of the snail (where she can rest, as necessary) and then out again without stepping on a line or putting down the other foot. If successful, she can choose one box to initial with chalk. This space then becomes her exclusive territory, which all other players must hop over, while she may use it as an additional resting spot. This makes the game more challenging as it progresses. Each player who completes a successful trip in and out of the snail can claim any free box with her initials. If a player steps on a line or puts her foot down or steps into an initialed box, play passes immediately to the next in line. The game continues until it is impossible for anyone to hop into the center space or until all spaces have someone's initials in them. The winner is the player with the most initialed spaces.

Chocolat Chaud (Hot Chocolate)

------

6 tablespoons unsweetened cocoa
6 tablespoons sugar
Pinch cinnamon
Pinch salt
5 cups milk
½ teaspoon vanilla extract

Mix cocoa, sugar, cinnamon, and salt in a small saucepan. Add two cups milk and heat on low to dissolve. Add the remaining milk, mix gently with a whisk, and heat not quite to boiling, stirring constantly so the milk doesn't scald. Stir in vanilla. Ladle into oversize cups. Serves two.

april
paloozas

Bonnets & Boxes

Whether you celebrate the Easter holiday or not, an Easter parade is an irresistible bit of fun for everyone. The grander-the-better bonnets parade along Fifth Avenue in New York on Easter Sunday is not to be missed.

Who can play?
All ages.

What do we need?
Old hats, party hats, paper and plastic hats from the party store, or a plain brown paper bag; plain hat-sized gift boxes with lids, wrapping paper or tissue paper; around-the-house and store-bought hat-and-box trimmings (feathers, buttons, ribbons, plastic fruits and gewgaws, sequins, glitter, and so on, needle, thread, scissors, and glue. Music from or videos of *Easter Parade, My Fair Lady,* or *Top Hat.*

Running time?
A couple of hours.

Budget?
$$

What's the Palooza?

This is a spring hat-making party, with an eye toward big, beautiful, startling, and surprising hats that make you click your heels that winter is over.

Merry Milliners and Mad Hatters

Rummage through your closets to find old hats of any kind—baseball caps, straw or Styrofoam boaters, winter knit caps, fedoras, and so on. You can also get paper or plastic hats of different styles at craft or party stores.

Make It a Party!

Invites: Make invitations shaped like different kinds of hats.

Food and Decor: Cover a large table with a brightly colored paper tablecloth for your hat factory. Display bowls filled with all kinds of hat-making trinkets, and arrange glue, scissors, needle, and thread all over the table for easy access. Serve snacks that inspire the milliners—colorful fruit salad, crazy gummy candies, nonpareils, M&Ms, marshmallows.

Activities: Make hats and hatboxes galore. Listen to the *My Fair Lady* sound track as you work. Award prizes in top hat categories such as Tallest Hat, Loudest Hat, Most Appetizing Hat, Best Historical Hat, Hairiest Hat. Take pictures of everyone wearing their hats. Watch *Easter Parade* or *My Fair Lady* for inspiration.

Favors: Take home your bonnet and box creations. Give out wrist pincushions and small sewing kits to the budding milliners.

Good Books

Try to find these books at the library. They're loaded with great information about the history of the hat, as well as hundreds of photos and illustrations of hats to inspire you. Check out *Hats* by Colin McDowell, *The Century of Hats* by Susie Hopkins, and *Classic Millinery Techniques: A Complete Guide to Making and Designing Today's Hats* by Ann Albrizio, Osnat Lustig, and Ted Morrison. Also look for my favorite: *Crowns: Portraits of Black Women in Church Hats* by Michael Cunningham and Craig Marberry. This delicious book is a must for would-be milliners, a celebration of the big hats the church ladies in Harlem wear every Sunday. A little bit of joy you wear on your head.

Pick a hat and dude it up! Use any kind of hat-trimming trinket to make your hat one-of-a-kind. Sew on buttons, ribbons, or feathers. Glue on sequins or glitter to up the sparkle factor. Make your own version of any kind of hat, from a plastic-fruit-covered Carmen Miranda hat to a winged Hermes helmet with feathers glued to cardboard cutouts. A Viking hat with ice cream cone horns. An Anne of Green Gables hat with two yarn braids attached under the brim. Make a Robin Hood hat out of felt and feather. Attach wire or pipe cleaners to the top of a colander for an alien space hat. Make a crown out of aluminum foil and shirt cardboard. Make a captain's hat with a star and gold braid out of a plain painter's cap.

To make a cheerful chapeau from scratch, start with a big brown paper bag. Crinkle it gently with your hands until it's soft and wrinkly, being careful not to rip the bag. Now decorate it with paint, feathers, ribbons,

What Hat Is That?

Beanie
Beret
Bonnet
Boater
Bowler
Busby
Cap
Cloche
Derby
Fedora
Fez
Homburg
Panama
Picture hat
Pillbox
Pith helmet
Porkpie
Shapka
Stetson
Stocking cap
Tam
Ten-gallon hat
Tricorner
Trilby
Top hat

buttons, lace, googly eyes, and so on. When you're finished (and it's completely dry), turn up the open end to form a brim. Put it on and take a twirl.

Hatboxes to Beat the Band

Make a hatbox to store your hat creation—or to stow your secret stuff! Decorate a plain hat-sized box and lid with paint, markers, and wrapping or tissue paper. Glue a ribbon around the belly of the box and another across or around the lid. Top it off with a big bow or a tissue-paper flower bouquet. Or cover the box in images clipped from magazines or from whimsical wrapping paper in the decoupage style.

Hattitudes

----

at the drop of a hat: Doing something impulsively.

eat my hat: Believe something is unlikely to happen.

hat in hand: Sheepishly begging for forgiveness.

hats off: Giving tribute, congratulating someone.

hat trick: A three-of-a-kind success, especially in hockey and soccer.

keep under your hat: Keep to yourself, keep secret.

old hat: Old-fashioned, passé.

pass the hat: Collect a contribution.

pick out of a hat: Choose at random.

pull the hat over your eyes: Fool someone.

talking through your hat: Speaking foolishness.

throw your hat in the ring: Take up a challenge, become a contender, usually political.

wear more than one hat: Play many roles at the same time.

Opening Day!

The World Series in October is great fun, but for the true fan, it's nothing compared to Opening Day of the baseball season. Like the crocuses peeking out of the snow in early spring, Opening Day signals the dawn of hope, a new beginning—it's the "next year" in "Just wait till next year!"

What's the Palooza?

Lots of favorite sports and pastimes have an opening day—and if yours doesn't, give it one! Make a big hoo-ha over the seasonal start of your favorite sport or hobby every year, and it will become one of your family's most important "holidays." One clan I know loves Opening Day of baseball season so much, they play hooky from work and school so they can be together to watch their team's first game. Sometimes they're able to score tickets to the game, sometimes they watch it from the couch in their living room; they don't care either way. Here are some ways you can make your Opening Day the best kind of tradition.

Tickets, Please

Make tickets on ticket-sized bits of paper marked with the details of your big game: "Admit One. Opening Day, April 7, 20XX. Tigers vs. Orioles. Gates open at 1:00." Use a hole punch along the edges of the ticket to give it that perforated look. Leave a blank line on the ticket where you can write the final score. Set a ticket by everyone's breakfast plate on the morning of Opening Day.

Who can play?
Ages 6 and up, or the whole family.

What do we need?
Paper, scissors, markers, and a single hole punch; plain T-shirts and fabric paint or pens; cake mix, cupcake liners, frosting, and decorating frosting; hot dogs and buns, root beer, peanuts in the shell or Cracker Jacks (or any other snacky treat that goes with your favorite activity); a camera.

Running time?
An hour or two, plus the time you spend watching the game.

Budget?
$$

Opening Day for baseball comes in the first week of April.

Baseball Cupcakes

Make cupcakes out of your favorite flavored. cake mix. When the cupcakes have cooled completely, frost them with white store-bought frosting and decorate half of them with red string licorice to look like the seams of a baseball. On the rest of the cupcakes, use colored cake decorator's frosting to create the logo of your favorite team.

T Time

On the eve of your Opening Day, make the ultimate collectible game-day T-shirt using a plain white or colored T-shirt and fabric paint or markers. Draw a picture of your favorite player—or the whole darn team! Mark the day and year somewhere on your shirt, for when you look back on your collection years from now. Invent your own slogans. One year a Green Bay Packers fan I know made himself a T-shirt that said simply, "Pack Attack," to commemorate the start of football season, and he wore the shirt every game day that season for good luck. In fact, he wore it for so many years it eventually just fell apart, but that's what fans do.

Team Picture

Take a family team picture, each of you wearing your custom-made Opening Day T-shirt, with bats and gloves and caps aplenty—or rods and reels and vests, as the case may be! You can also take pictures of each person to create trading cards, with funny statistics, nicknames, or little personality profiles on the back.

Play-by-Play

If you're watching a game on television, turn down the sound and practice your play-by-play announcing. There's a trick to it, of course. You have to be paying careful attention to who's playing on both teams, what's happening on the field, and what the official's calls are (according to their hand signals, which you need to be familiar with). The best radio announcers know that clearly describing what's happening on the field should allow the listeners to visualize the game. Too much silly chatter between the announcers can get in the way of that, but not enough friendly talk can make a game sound as interesting as watching paint dry. Get whipped up with enthusiam for the big plays. Come up with a signature line—Chicago's beloved Harry Caray was famous for "Holy cow!" and "It could be . . . it might be . . . it is! A home run!!!" And don't forget to do your homework. Find interesting information about the players and the game to bring to your announcing, so you can fill the time between at-bats or during commercials. That'll keep your listeners coming back for more.

Fan Fare

Serve snacks in a shoe box for the bleacher creatures (popcorn or Cracker Jacks in a cup, hot dog on a bun, soda in a can) or make it slick for the swanks in the skybox (sausage and peppers in a crusty roll, gourmet chips, and flavored seltzer water). Serve a pile of Baseball Cupcakes.

Fish Fan

Fisherpeople may be even more avid than baseball fans when it comes to Opening Day. Lots of them like to camp out near the place they want to fish so that they're there, renewed fishing license in hand, ready for the first possible moment of Opening-Day fishing. Anglers, like hunters, love being at the starting gate of their season, no matter how ungodly the hour. Every state has different rules and dates for Opening Day, and often Opening Day for one kind of fish (say, trout) is different than for another kind of fish (like walleye), but most openers take place somewhere between early April and late May. Some states allow fishing year-round, in which case many fishing fans create a kind of personal Opening Day, a day in March, perhaps, when the water's warmed up just enough to be bearable for wading. For just about every angler, though, Opening Day of fishing season is the true beginning of spring.

Mona Lisa

Is that a smile on your face? The allure of the most famous painting in the world is worth pondering any day of the year, but especially on Leonardo da Vinci's birthday.

Who can play?

Ages 6 and up.

What do we need?

Art supplies for painting, coloring, or otherwise rendering a Mona Lisa reproduction, including canvas or heavy-duty drawing paper, acrylic paints, watercolors, crayons, or pastels; computer with Internet access; writing instruments and paper.

Running time?

Two hours or more, depending on activities you choose.

Budget?

$$

What's the Palooza?

Consider the *Mona Lisa* in all her glory and devise your own interpretation of the painting. Whether you decide to create a faithful reproduction (okay, well, maybe not *so* faithful) or a wholly original twist on Leonardo's theme or whether you invent your own back story or write and perform a Mona Lisa monologue, this palooza explores the painted lady in all her guises and disguises and lets us appreciate all over again the masterpiece that she is.

Paint Your Own

Choose your medium and make a replica of Leonardo da Vinci's celebrated *Mona Lisa*. The actual *Mona Lisa* was created using oil paint on wood, but you might try acrylic paints on canvas or heavy drawing paper. You could also use watercolors or even pastels. Start by having a good long look at da Vinci's masterpiece—you can see it at http://www.ibiblio.org/wm/paint/auth/vinci/joconde/ or in many art history books at the library, such as Janson's *History of Art for Young People* or *The Annotated Mona Lisa* by Carol Strickland and John Boswell.

Leonardo first drew the shape or outline of his portrait before filling it in with oils. You can go to www.enchantedlearning.com/artists/davinci/coloring/

monalisa.shtml to print out a coloring outline of *Mona Lisa,* which may help you with the proportions and general outline of your portrait. As he worked, da Vinci thinned the oil paint so that it could actually be applied like a glaze, allowing him to do layer upon layer, re-working the subtleties of his subject's face. The result is an exquisite mystery in her expression, a quality schol-ars have said Leonardo achieved through light and shadows and lines that never allow the viewer's eye to rest on any one part of her face, much less decide for certain whether the portrait depicts a smile or some-thing else.

As you create your *Mona Lisa,* refer frequently to the details of the original painting—her expression, the light on her sleeves, the ornamentation around the neck-line of her dress, the geography in the background—and approximate whatever you can in your own picture. By the time you are done, you'll see that your painting is its own original piece of art, a little like the original, and full of a new appreciation of the genius of da Vinci's work.

Leonardo da Vinci's birthday is April 15, 1452.

Defining da Vinci

For a fellow who is believed to have completed only six paintings in his lifetime, Leonardo da Vinci sure turned the art world upside down. His work was so unique that they literally did not have words to describe it. In the end, they had to invent one: *sfumato,* from an Italian word that means "turned to mist." This referred to da Vinci's ability to create minute and delicate shifts between color areas, causing a kind of smoky effect. It is why *Mona Lisa* is such a lovely mystery to the millions of people who have stood before her over the last five centuries—and why no painter was ever truly able to copy da Vinci or turn his technique into a style for others to follow. Even da Vinci himself thought it was a neat trick; he liked his *Mona Lisa* so much, he carried it around with him from city to city for ten years after he finished the painting in 1506, finally selling it to the king of France to hang in his castle at Ambroise.

Iconography

When an image is so familiar that it's famous for being famous, it has become an *icon,* or a symbol. The United States flag and Uncle Sam are icons, for example. A sure sign that an image has become an icon is when people other than the original artist create alternate interpretations of the image. As the most widely recognized and celebrated painting in the history of art, *Mona Lisa* is the definition of an icon. Her image is used freely on everything from shower curtains to Post-it notes. The *Mona Lisa* has been endlessly reinterpreted by other artists, perhaps most notably by Marcel Duchamp, who

Make It a Party!

- - - - - - -

Invites: *Mona Lisa* postcards, of course.

Food and Decor: Leonardo was a vegetarian whose favorite meal was minestrone soup. Serve that if your party includes lunch or dinner, along with crusty bread and olive oil for dipping. Gelato or spumoni for dessert. Flowers on the table. *Mona Lisa* posters. For tunes, make sure you have Nat King Cole's "Mona Lisa," a number-one hit in 1950. And, of course, Seal's "Mona Lisa Smile," and the rest of the sound track from the movie of the same name.

Activities: Have a make-your-own-*Mona Lisa* paint-a-thon. Give each guest a 2-by-3-foot sheet of sturdy art paper and a *Mona Lisa* coloring outline to use as a guide. Have *Mona Lisa* posters in easy view and paint away! You could also have a variety of other kinds of materials available to create alternative-style *Mona Lisas,* such as pipe cleaners for a pop-art *Mona Lisa* or multicolored scraps of tissue paper to create an abstract collage.

And don't forget to have a backward writing challenge. Leonardo is famous for the backward writing, or mirror writing, in his many journals. Some say he did it because he was secretive and wanted to hide his ideas from prying eyes. Others say it was just because he was a clever fellow with a nimble mind and a true lefty's desire not to smudge ink across the page as he wrote! Teach yourself to write your name backward as easily as you ordinarily write it. Have everyone write a backward journal entry and illustrate it with pencil sketches in the margin like the master. To see a snip of Leonardo's backward writing in his journal, go to http://www.amnh.org/exhibitions/codex/2A2r.html.

Favors: *Mona Lisa* trinkets. Journals and pencils. Paperback edition of *The Second Mrs. Giaconda* by E. L. Konigsburg.

gave the little lady a mustache and a goatee in his notorious rendering *LHOOQ* in 1919. Other reinterpretations include Andy Warhol's *Two Golden Mona Lisas,* which featured silkscreened dual images of *Mona Lisa,* and Fernando Botero's *Mona Lisa,* which is similar to the original in composition, but features a roly-poly round-faced Mona Lisa, in the classic Botero style.

Create your own unique interpretation of the painting. If you're a New York Yankees fan, perhaps your Mona wears a baseball cap? How about Mona Lisa frowning? Or Mona Lisa laughing. Hip-hop Mona Lisa? Yo.

Who's That Lady?

Was Mona Lisa the wife of Florentine merchant Francesco del Giacondo, or is she da Vinci himself in self-portrait? Scholars have floated all kinds of theories about the identity of Mona Lisa, and to this day no one version is proven. *The Second Mrs. Giaconda* is popular children's author E. L. Konigsburg's lively imagining of the story behind Leonardo's *Mona Lisa.* Make up your own backstory to the painting. Who is Mona Lisa? What is her relationship to the artist? Why did he paint her?

Mona Lisa Monologue

Pretend you're the painted lady hanging in the Louvre in Paris. If you could suddenly come to life and address the tourists standing around your bulletproof glass box, what would you say to them? Write a monologue or poem from Mona Lisa's point of view. Or choose another image from a famous painting and write from its point of view: How about Botticelli's Venus? What is that lady from Grant Wood's *American Gothic* thinking anyway? What if Whistler's mother could give us a piece of her mind?

The eyes have the luster and moisture always seen in living people, while around them are the lashes and all the reddish tones which cannot be produced without the greatest care. The eyebrows could not be more natural. . . . The nose seems lifelike with its beautiful pink and tender nostrils. The mouth, with its opening joining the red of the lips to the flesh of the face, seems to be real flesh rather than paint. Anyone who looked very attentively at the hollow of her throat would see her pulse beating.

—Giorgio Vasari (1511–1574), a Florentine painter said to be the first art historian, on viewing *Mona Lisa*

Make a Date with a Mona Lisa

The *Mona Lisa* isn't just the most famous painting in the world, it's also the most visited. Nearly six million people a year come to the Louvre museum, many of them just to see her! That's a long way to go (and a mighty big crowd to fight!) just to see one painting. But I do love the idea of going to a museum to spend a little quality time with just one piece of art. Research what special paintings or pieces of art are in the museums closest to where you live. Choose one with which to have a little "art date." Read up on the piece and on the artist. Find out where in the museum the piece is displayed. Plan to go at a time when the museum isn't at its busiest—a weekday morning is ideal. Then show up and take the time to enjoy all the special details of this single piece of art.

One, Two, Tree

Every Arbor Day, I am reminded of two of my favorite family photos; one is my sister—tiny at the time—planting an acorn with my grandmother. The other is a photo from forty years later, a shot of the towering oak tree that acorn had become. It's Arbor Day! Measure yourself against your favorite tree. And don't forget to plant one!

What's the Palooza?

Find the art in the trees and trees in the art. Sculptor Andy Goldsworthy finds all the tools and materials he needs for his art in the great outdoors: icicles, mud, twigs, thorns, leaves, grasses, moss, stones, and rocks, even sheep's wool. Some of his most breathtaking sculptures are found in trees—a tree limb highlighted with a long line of dandelions; branches wrapped in red poppy petals; tree trunks outlined with white sheep's wool. Goldsworthy balances perfect snowballs in the notches of wet, black branches; he uses thorns to pin scarlet maple leaves in a V pattern between tree trunks. Some of his sculptures last just minutes. Others blow away, back into nature, into the air or water, over weeks and months.

Who can play?
All ages.

What do we need?
Camera, tape recorder or CD player, shallow cardboard box, and picnic fixings.

Running time?
One to two hours.

Budget?
Free.

Artful Forest

Gather as many bright yellow dandelion heads—or fallen dogwood, tulip, or other spring petals—as you can find on the ground. Look for an empty tree hole or crevice and stuff it with the dandelion buds or flower petals until it is jammed with color. Is that not gor-

National Arbor Day is the last Friday in April.

Worth a Look

Check out Andy Goldsworthy's extra-ordinary art in his book *Wood,* or at www.smithsonian magazine.si.edu/ smithsonian/issues97/ feb97/golds.html.

geous? Photograph your arrangement. Or line up the dandelion heads or flower petals along the length of a tree branch and take a picture of the colorful flower buds or petals against the bark. Goldsworthy exhibits photos like these in museums all over the world.

Look for interesting shapes and angles in large fallen branches in the woods. Drag one to a clearing, arrange it in an interesting way, and photograph it. Adorn it with other natural elements like acorns, rocks, or leaves you find nearby to compose a still life. Or take the branch to an entirely different place for a creative setting for your sculpture. Picture *Pine Bough on a Pontiac* or *Limb of a Mighty Oak on Asphalt*. A white-barked aspen or birch branch against a lush green meadow, well, you can practically charge admission to look at that!

Stick Throw

Andy Goldsworthy once photographed a dozen or so dancers from the French avant-garde Ballet Atlantique as they performed a "Stick Throw" in Scotland. Go to www.getty.edu/artsednet/images/Ecology/ballet.html to see the photo, with dancers silhouetted against a clouded sky. Choreograph and photograph your own Stick Throw. Collect armfuls of lightweight sticks and twigs. One person is assigned to photograph the freeform

Missing Trees

It's funny how Arbor Day got its start on the treeless plains of Nebraska. In the 1800s, Nebraska settlers from the East missed their trees, with the spring flowers, cheap wood for fuel, building materials, windbreaks, and shade. No trees to climb, no cool place to picnic. These people needed trees, and a newspaperman, J. Sterling Morton, thought of a way to get a lot of them. In 1872, he suggested a tree-planting holiday called Arbor Day. Nebraskans planted more than a million trees on that first Arbor Day, April 10, 1872. Now the whole country observes Arbor Day on the last Friday in April, or during the best tree-planting weather. You can find out when your state celebrates Arbor Day by visiting arbor-day.org and get ten free trees if you become a member.

ballet to the sounds of music like Beethoven's *Pastoral* Symphony or Aaron Copland's *Appalachian Spring*. Everyone else dances to the music in a long line, each dancer arm's distance apart and carrying an armful of lightweight sticks. When the photographer yells, "Throw!" performers toss their sticks up in the air (out and away from the dance line!), arms extended, as the photographer snaps. End of ballet! Rehearse the dance and the stick throw in advance, to iron out the kinks, and to give the photographer a sense of where his best shot will be.

arboretum, n.: A tree garden.

Stick Ball

Gather up your sticks from Stick Throw and arrange them in interesting formations like domes, nests, wreaths, patterns, or Stick Balls, round sculptures made entirely of sticks. If you have a day, a lot of sticks, and *a lot* of patience, like Andy Goldsworthy, you can make a Stick Ball by s-l-o-w-l-y arranging sticks, stick by stick, into a round or oval form. But with a little mud and maybe some leaves, acorns, and seeds, you can shape a Stick Ball that will really stick together. Assemble your Stick Ball near a tree or in the middle of an open space, the way Andy does. Or make yours inside a shoe-box lid or shallow box to carry home.

Grow Your Own

Tree farmer and historian Jeff Meyer is renowned for growing trees from seeds or cuttings from famous and historic trees, like the honey locust under which Abraham Lincoln gave the Gettysburg Address or the pin oak that grows in front of Elvis Presley's Graceland mansion. Meyer, founder of America's Famous & Historic Trees Project, is known as the modern-day Johnny Appleseed, and no wonder; he's planted more than a million trees himself, most of them grown by him from seed. He swears growing a tree from seed is as easy as apple pie. Go to www.historictrees.org/howtogrow for simple instructions on growing apple, oak, maple, and walnut trees from seed. All you have to do is collect the seeds in the fall, store them over the winter, and plant them in the springtime—and *voilà!* you're a tree farmer! Plant a tree every year and in fifteen years, you can have an Arbor Day picnic with your family under your own little grove of homegrown oak or apple trees.

Tree Travel

You don't have to go to the forest to see the trees. Visit the amazing Sequoia National Park online at www.sequoianationalpark.org. There you'll find the world's largest living thing, the Sherman Tree, a giant sequoia. And get a look at Tunnel Log, another giant sequoia you can drive right through. Also visit the Web site for American Forests, this country's oldest conservation group (www.americanforests.org), and check out their Big Tree program, which is a registry of the biggest trees in the country, searchable by location and species. If you live near a tree that you think should be a champ, this Web site will tell you how to measure it and nominate it for consideration.

Trees are poems that earth writes upon the sky.

—Kahlil Gibran (1883–1931)

may
paloozas

Tunnels

Some people want to fly through the clouds, some want to tunnel to the center of the earth. This palooza is for the tunnelers.

Who can play?
Ages 9 and up.

What do we need?
Three feet or more of 6-inch wide plastic tubing (PVC), wide plumber's tubing, or plastic gutter, all with elbow pieces, as necessary (you can find these at Home Depot), scrap pieces of plywood sized to support as you dig, and a shovel. Hand auger optional.

Running time?
A couple of hours (or months, for a great escape!).

Budget?
$$

What's the Palooza?

Build a little tunnel—then try to stop dreaming about digging a big professional one! How amazing is a tunnel? Think of all the human ingenuity, precise engineering, and backbreaking labor it takes to make one. It's taken thousands of years to perfect the art of building tunnels, but it all comes down to three steps:

1. Excavate—dig through the earth to make way for the tunnel.
2. Build a support structure—this is to make the environment stable while the tunnel is constructed.
3. Line it—install a lining for the tunnel that is appropriate for its intended use.

Since you're not licensed to use explosives or operate a rock borer(!) you won't be building a rock tunnel. And I'm fairly certain Mom and Dad won't want you to build a water tunnel your first time out. So you'll likely be building a soft-ground tunnel, by digging a trench, dropping in your tunnel lining, and backfilling with soil to cover the tunnel. This basic method is called *cut-and-cover*, and is how most sewer or electrical lines are installed.

You might also use a hand auger (if you happen to have one in the garage). This is a cool tool with a crank handle on one end and rotating corkscrew-like blades at the bottom. When you dig with an auger, the blades cut up and lift out the dirt when you remove the auger from the hole. So you dig a little, remove the soil, dig a little more, remove more soil, and so on.

Whether you're using a shovel or an auger or both, you have to find a good spot for your little tunnel. Inspect your yard for a place where a) you're allowed to dig(!), b) you'll have clearance from one end to the other to lay your piping, and c) there's space for the tunnel openings at both ends. If you have a limited digging space, cut your piping down to fit.

You'll want to use the cut-and-cover method for a horizontal tunnel, perhaps along with a bit of auger-style dig-and-remove. Either way, you need to insert plywood supports as you dig so the surrounding soil doesn't collapse in on your hole. Dig at least four inches deeper than the diameter of your piping so that after you backfill with soil, your tunnel will be invisible except at either end. When you've dug the desired depth and length of your tunnel, install your lining, making sure you've left a little plastic overhang on the top of each end of the lining to prevent the soil from

falling back into the tunnel. This is called a *tunnel shield* and all soft-ground tunnels have them. Finally, backfill with soil. Tamp the soil gently with your feet to firm it up, than cover it with grass clippings or hay. This is, of course, to camouflage your brand new, secret underground tunnel!

If you have a guinea pig or hamster, he might have a little fun exploring your tunnel (have a second person at the other end so he doesn't scurry off into the wilderness!). Or you can play with cars or action figures

The Chunnel (Channel Tunnel) that links England and the European continent opened on May 6, 1994.

in the tunnel, or see how well you constructed your tunnel by shooting water through with a hose.

A Backyard Burrow

A friend of mine spent an entire summer of her childhood building an underground tunnel fort with five neighborhood friends. There was a big potato field behind their houses, so they had access to great, diggable dirt and few rocks at the edge of the field. They had no plan and no idea how to build a tunnel, but

Tunnel Tales

The Chunnel is what they call the thirty-two-mile rail tunnel that runs below the English Channel, connecting England with France. Opened in 1994, it took giant tunnel boring machines working from both directions three years to finally meet in the middle of the English Channel. Made of steel and concrete, the Chunnel consists of two full-size rail tunnels and a smaller emergency tunnel that runs between them. Rent *Chunnel: The Modern Marvels* and watch the Discovery Channel's amazing *Extreme Engineering* series to see firsthand how the Chunnel, as well as other astounding tunnels, were constructed.

Journey to the Center of the Earth, Jules Verne's 1868 classic novel, is considered the first science adventure story and the beginning of the genre we know as *sci-fi.* All these years later, it's as exciting a story as ever, with three men fixated on their search for the mysterious center of the earth. They begin their odyssey by going down into a dormant volcano, and trek toward the earth's crust through perilous tunnels and caverns, with countless chilling dangers along the way. Read this book—or build a blanket tunnel in your room to lie inside while you listen to it on tape.

The Great Escape is a movie (based on a true story) about a group of Allied Royal Air Force officers who are imprisoned at a German prisoner of war camp during World War II. These men create an elaborate escape plan that requires them to dig their way to freedom, handful by handful of dirt, building one of the longest, most cleverly conceived tunnels ever made.

The Big Dig is the nickname for Boston's Central Artery/Tunnel Project, described as "the largest, most complex, and technologically challenging highway project in American history. And it was *big*. Nearly fourteen years in the making, this tunnel system essentially reinvented traffic in the city of Boston. Go to *www.bigdig.com* to see photographs and videoclips of all the different stages of construction, as well as pictures of the cool archeological artifacts they found when they were digging.

they had six shovels and all the time in the world so they just started digging. They dug a hole about six feet deep and wide, and then began digging a horizontal opening about four feet tall and wide. Soon they realized that if they didn't do something to shore up the roof and sides the soil would collapse. So they foraged for scrap plywood in their garages and used it to build supporting walls and a ceiling as they progressed. They also eventually figured out that they needed a plywood overhang on both ends to keep the soil from slipping back into the tunnel (having discovered, without engineering degrees, the need for a tunnel shield!). By the time the summer was over, their hands were covered with calluses, but the tunnel fort was finished. It had an entrance and an exit, a little (very little!) bench for seating, and a sign outside that said, of course, "Keep Out!" Unfortunately, the tunnel could only hold a couple of people at a time, so after months of teamwork and togetherness, the six diggers ended the summer bickering over whose turn it was to play in the tunnel fort.

Light at the end of the tunnel, n. phrase: A feeling of hope and relief that a long journey or difficult effort is almost over.

Baby Day

Nothing tickles me more than the arrival of a new baby on the scene. I loved when each of my own kids arrived; now just about any newborn can put a goofy grin on my face. This palooza is a shameless excuse to spend a happy bit of time with whatever new baby enters your orb.

What's the Palooza?

When a new baby comes along (in your own family or a friend's), have a "laughing party" to give the newbie a big, happy howdy-do.

Laugh Along

There's a wonderful Navajo tradition called *chi dlo dil* that calls for whoever is the first to make a new baby laugh to host a celebration for the baby and his/her parents. Because most babies begin smiling and laughing from the age of six weeks on, the laughing party usually takes place around this time. Plan for a party in your home or volunteer to bring the party to the new baby's home (whichever is most appealing to the new baby's parents). This isn't a shower; no one needs to bring gifts of Snugglies or onesies or Diaper Genies. This is a welcoming party for baby with homemade gifts and good wishes from each guest for the baby.

Lullaby

This is something special for you to create for a new baby, a secret gift between you and her. Listen to some classic lullabies or quiet children's tunes for ideas to create an original lullaby. Lullabies are simple, soothing songs meant to calm a baby or help her relax and go to sleep. These songs often feature the repetition of gentle tunes and phrases, creating a soft rhythm that can be calming to the baby.

Your song doesn't have to be a Rock-a-Bye-Baby song that's *about* going to sleep; it can be about anything you want. Maybe a little song about animals or colors or things a baby likes to do. One friend of mine turned the usually rollicking "She'll Be Coming Round the Mountain" into a slow, funny lullaby with new lyrics for her baby son. Or look at storybooks for inspiration—can you turn *Goodnight Moon* into a lullaby? Feel free to use the tunes from familiar lullabies or songs and adapt them with your own words and variations. Then the first chance you get to have a quiet moment with the new baby, whisper your lullaby gift in her ear.

German composer Johannes Brahms was born on May 7, 1833.

Baby Book

This is a fun gift to make for a new baby. Write a nutty story or narrative poem in which the baby is the star— *Baby Tales* or *Baby Joey's Outrageous Adventure*. The crazier and more unlikely the story, the funnier it is that your baby is the star. Illustrate your story, leaving spaces to glue different photos of the baby in the various scenes. Or make and illustrate a book of your favorite silly jokes. Check out *Bed! Bed! Bed!* a book and CD combination by quirky rockers They Might Be Giants, for inspiration.

Good Advice

Write down the numbers 1 to 18 on small pieces of paper and drop them in baby's hat. Have each party guest pick a number from the hat. Hand out pieces of paper and writing utensils

Golden Lullabies

The Standards

"All the Pretty Horses"

"Are You Sleeping?"

"Brahms Lullaby"

"Golden Slumbers"

"Hush Little Baby"

"Rock-a-Bye Baby"

"Sleep, Baby, Sleep"

"Twinkle, Twinkle, Little Star"

The Contemporaries

"Child of Mine," Carole King

"Isn't She Lovely," Stevie Wonder

"Beautiful Boy," John Lennon

"You Are the Love of My Life," Carly Simon

"Baby, Baby," Amy Grant

"Lullaby (Goodnight My Angel)," Billy Joel

and have guests write a bit of useful advice for the child, to be read on the birthday of the age/number. The advice can be funny or serious, any way you want to play it. It can be one word or a sentence of advice, or a whole letter. Someone I know wrote a letter to a newborn baby telling him funny things about his parents he'd be glad to know when he got older. Read all the advice aloud at your laughing party.

Brahms Lullaby

Although Johannes Brahms was one of the world's greatest classical composers, he may be best known as the man who wrote the timeless lullaby originally called "Cradle Song," but now known simply as "Brahms' Lullaby." He wrote the song to celebrate the birth of a friend's child. He told his friends he wrote the song by remembering a tune sung to him by a long-ago love. Little did he know his lullaby love song would become the granddaddy of all lullabies, the gently swaying tune by which all other lullabies would be measured. Loosely translated from the German, here are the lyrics:

Lullaby and good night, with roses bedight,*
With lilies o'er spread is baby's wee bed.
Lay thee down now and rest, may thy slumber be blessed.
Lay thee down now and rest, may thy slumber be blessed.

Lullaby and good night, thy mother's delight,
Shining angels beside my darling abide.
They will guard thee at rest, thou shalt wake on my breast.
They will guard thee at rest, thou shalt wake on my breast.

* bedight (v.): decorate, dress up.

Bull Day

"Happiness is the china shop; love is the bull," said American writer H. L. Mencken. Like a bull in a china shop. Sure, the bull has that knocking-stuff-over-and-breaking-it-into-smithereens reputation, but he's also strong! Dependable! Keen-witted! You want him in your corner when things get tricky. The same can be said of people born under the sign of Taurus, the Bull.

What's the Palooza?

The bull. Feared for its fiery unpredictability, admired for its full-force strength and determination. The ancient Egyptians believed the bull to be the incarnation of Ptah, the creator of the universe and great decision maker of destiny, and they celebrated a seven-day-long Festival of the Bull to honor this mighty animal. No gesture is too grand when feting a Taurean—they are by nature great believers in all the pleasure that life has to offer, epicureans in the Greek tradition. Begin the festivities in grand style with a little parade, much like the procession that began the great festival. Have the birthday guests hold up red bandannas tied to wooden paint stirrers and wave them in the air as they make a circuitous route to party headquarters.

Taking the Horns with the Bull

The phrase "take the bull by the horns" means to boldly confront a difficult situation. It comes from a Spanish proverb that, translated, states that one should "take a bull by the horn and a man at his word." So every Taur-

---

Who can play?

Ages 9 and up.

What do we need?

Wooden paint stirrers and red bandannas; wide plastic headbands, bakeable Sculpey clay, acrylic paint, glitter and glue, superglue or two-part epoxy; 13 pieces of shirt cardboard, markers, and checkers' sawhorses and a 5-to-8-foot rope.

Running time?

One and a half to two hours.

Budget?

$$

People whose birthdays are between April 20 and May 20 fall under the zodiac sign of Taurus, the Bull.

baby should have his own personal set of horns to match his bull-headed personality. To make the horns, take a fistful of Sculpey baking clay, roll out a fat cylinder, divide it in two, and form horn-shaped pieces. Shape the bottom of the horns by pressing them flat against the top of a plastic headband (where they will eventually be attached). Bake according to the Sculpey package directions, cool completely, then decorate them any way you like, with acrylic paint, glue and glitter, or any other razzle-dazzle. After your horns are dry, attach them to the headband with superglue or two-part epoxy, carefully following package directions. After the glue dries completely, don your horns and take a group picture of a whole bunch of bulls.

Two Truths and a Lie

When someone tells you a cock-and-bull story, they're probably lying. This phrase comes from an old English legend of two inns in the tiny village of Stony Stratford, the Cock and the Bull, where wild and extravagant

Make It a Party!

Invites: Print some cool images of bulls from the Internet and make a bull collage around the edges of a piece of paper. "We're Bullish on Megan's 12th Birthday! Come celebrate with our favorite Taurean!"

Food and Decor: Decorate with anything red—streamers, handkerchiefs, balloons; red paper plates, napkins, and cups. A few bull's-eyes hung on the walls would be witty. Taureans love their food, so make it a tasty spread of favorite dishes. And don't forget the bull's sweet tooth—treats made with marshmallows, cinnamon, and especially mint chocolate will hit the spot.

Activities: Make horns, play Two Truths and a Lie, make and play a Minotaur game, head outside for a bit of bull jumping.

Favors: Headband horns; spicy Red Hots, mint Hershey's Kisses, anything with the Chicago Bulls or Texas Longhorns logo on it; all wrapped up hobo-style in a red bandanna.

traveler's tales were often told. Play a game in which you must tell two truths and a lie about yourself, and see if your guests can guess which ones are which. Think of little-known or hard-to-believe facts about your childhood history, a family story, or a place or time that your friends didn't know you. Then throw in a lie that could pass as a truth. Go around in a circle, collecting each person's guess. Every person who guesses correctly gets a point. For every person who guesses incorrectly, the storyteller gets a point. Move around the circle in order, each person telling their two truths and a lie. The person with the most points at the end of all the tall tales wins.

sun sign, n.: Refers to one of the twelve signs of the zodiac that the sun was in at the time of your birth. To say, "I am a Taurus," is to say, I was born during the time of year that the sun passes through the sign of Taurus.

Lost in the Labyrinth

In Greek mythology, the Minotaur was half bull, half man, the offspring of Queen Pasiphae, whose husband was King Minos. Minos confined the Minotaur to a labyrinth from which escape was impossible, built beneath the castle of Knossos. Every nine years, seven young men and seven maidens were sent into the labyrinth as a sacrifice to the hungry beast. That is, until Athenian hero Theseus entered the Labyrinth and slayed the Minotaur. The Minotaur is one of the favorite bad guys of all mythology—he appears in centuries of ancient art and literature, in a board game discovered in Crete dating back to around 1000 B.C., and all the way to the present, where he's the star of countless video and computer games.

Make your own Labyrinth of Minotaur game, inspired by Toby Nelson's *Mad Mazes,* a book of make-your-own mazes. Ours is a two-player game where one person is Theseus, and the other is the Minotaur. Using markers and pieces of shirt cardboard, create a series of thirteen simple mazes (see samples below) on a 6-by-6 grid of 2-inch boxes. Each maze has only one opening through which Theseus (the black checker) can escape. The Minotaur (the red checker)

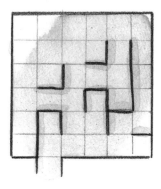

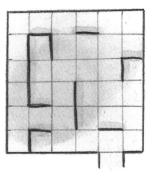

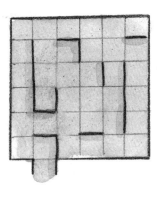

is positioned somewhere near the exit, waiting for Theseus.

The rules are simple. For each turn that Theseus takes, the Minotaur takes two turns. For his first turn, Minotaur will move one square horizontally, if this is possible. For his second turn, he tries to move one square vertically, also if possible. If he is unable to move either horizontally or vertically, Minotaur must skip his turn. For his turn, Theseus can move one square in any direction he likes. The idea is to anticipate the Minotaur's moves and create move strategies to avoid being captured. The key is to remember that Minotaur moves horizontally first, then vertically. When Theseus successfully makes it out of the maze, he wins. If the Minotaur moves onto the space where Theseus sits, well, let's just say Theseus is lunch.

When you finish with one maze, pass it on to the next pair of players and pick up a new maze to play. Winner is the player in each pairing with the most wins. You can also have a tournament where the winner of each pairing goes on to play the other winners, until there are just two left to play a championship, and then one, the big winner, who is the Lord or Lady of the Labyrinth.

Bullgames

Bull pen, bull's-eye, and *bullhorn* are some of the sports terms associated with the word *bull*. But what about bull jumping? This ancient white-knuckle sport actually involved real bulls. Participants in this acrobatic test of wills would launch themselves over the horns and body of a moving bull, to the cheers of a thrilled crowd. Set up a couple of sawhorses outdoors, securing them at the feet with rocks or bricks to keep them steady. Hold a bull-jumping contest involving a series of increasingly challenging jumps over the sawhorses. Also in the spirit of bull jumping, play Swing the Shoe, which involves tying somebody's shoe to the end of a rope (between five and eight feet long) and spinning it around in a circle.

Players must jump over the rope as it passes them without hitting their feet or legs. If they do, they're out. The last person standing and still jumping is the winner. To make the game more challenging, swing the shoe faster so it goes higher.

The Fiesta was going on outside in the night but I was too sleepy for it to keep me awake. When I woke it was the sound of the rocket exploding that announced the release of the bulls from the corrals at the edge of town. They would race through the streets and out to the bull-ring, . . . Down below the streets were empty. All the balconies were crowded with people. Suddenly a crowd came down the street. They were all running, packed close together. . . . Behind them was a little bare space, and then the bulls, galloping, tossing their heads up and down. It all went out of sight around the corner. One man fell, rolled to the gutter, and lay quiet. But the bulls went right on and did not notice him. They were all running together.

—Ernest Hemingway, *The Sun Also Rises*

Celebrate Any Sign

It doesn't matter whether you believe in astrology or not—you can party like a Taurean no matter what sign of the zodiac you are! Adapt activities and party details to each sign, making the most of the sign's symbol, and with emphasis on a few specifics, as follows. For the person born under the sign of:

Aries (March 21 to April 19): A party for the Ram calls for mad dashes and bursts of active entertainment, perhaps charades, a scavenger hunt, and a funky, frantic relay race. The Aries likes variety, so put out a spread of different snacky, occasionally spicy appetizers. Scary stories and suspenseful movies appeal to the Aries (think Stephen King or M. Night Shyamalan), so an adrenaline-rushing, movie-watching slumber party would make him happy.

Gemini (May 21 to June 21): The Gemini Twins like to have it both ways; good-quality food, but make it snappy. Silly comedy and serious nonfiction. The Goo-Goo Dolls and Gregorian chants. Make your party a mix of frothy fun and brainy challenge, a grab bag of music and food, and games or sports played in pairs.

Cancer (June 22 to July 22): The sensitive, caring Cancer the Crab loves hearth and home. Comfort food, cozy music or movies, classic TV shows—all this appeals to the Crab. Put together a sleepover party involving these things—making homemade pizza, dancing to the Beatles, playing a TV trivia game, watching *Little Women* or *Sleepless in Seattle*. Water sports or games on a warm, sunny day will make her smile, too.

Leo (July 23 to August 22): Leo the Lion lives for high drama and instant excitement. Rousing games and activities where the Leo is the leader are a good idea—he likes to compete, and he likes his team to win. There's a reason the lion is the symbol of royalty; like the Leo, a king wants the best of everything. An elaborate birthday cake from the best bakery in town; tasty, authentic food made with the best ingredients; that brand of incredible ginger ale that's impossible to find. Go all out for the Leo—he'll totally appreciate it.

Virgo (August 23 to September 22): The Virgo maiden loves beauty and order. She's got good taste, but she's practical and wouldn't appreciate anything that's unnecessarily frivolous or nutty. Fun for a Virgo is solving a puzzle or making something lovely but useful. So games that make her feel she's solved or accomplished something are in order, as are crafts like making and decorating a picture frame—or even better, little boxes she can use to organize things. Virgo won't eat just anything, so be sure to serve only her particular favorites.

Libra (September 23 to October 22): Libra, the Scales, likes things to be balanced and fair. So games where everyone's a winner or sports of individual accomplishment like gymnastics or ice-skating are appealing. Libras are fun to surprise, because they are happy with whatever is presented to them. Movies or stories where everything works out in the end, a friendly mix of music (nothing too extreme), a nice meal at a pleasantly set table—that's the ticket.

Scorpio (October 23 to November 21): Scorpio, the Scorpion, has a curious mind and enjoys games and sports that require thinking and strategizing—chess, flag football, or tricky treasure hunts, perhaps. Anything involving mysteries of all kinds—from ghost tales to detective stories to UFO accounts—sounds like a good time to a Scorpio. He's also attracted to intense flavors, so tickle his fancy with Indian or Thai foods.

Sagittarius (November 22 to December 21): Sagittarius, the Archer, loves travel, adventure, and new experiences. Put together action-packed games from other lands—an Italian Palio-style competion, a wilderness Survivor-style game, a Tour de France or Iditarod-style race. The Sag loves stories and music of other cultures, the sound of foreign languages, and exotic foods. Serve up a bit of all of it!

Capricorn (December 22 to January 19): On the one hand, Capricorn, the Goat, is fascinated by obscure products, bizarre animals and artifacts and offbeat stories. On the other, she's down-to-earth and practical always striving for self-improvement. Find ways to mix it up—a spa party, with facials using exotic ingredients or ancient methods (stones, mud, aromas). A visit to the natural history museum to look at bones or the reptile zoo to spend time with the slitherers. Serve down-home food, though, whatever you do.

Aquarius (January 20 to February 18): Aquarius, the Water Bearer, is interested in all things unusual and scientific. Games or outings relating to the future or science fiction are ideal. Extreme sports and activities like snowboarding or surfing hit the spot. Though the Aquarian is partial to strong flavors and he'll try just about anything, he's not fussy about what he eats, so don't knock yourself out trying to dazzle. He will appreciate, however, any food or decor that plays off his favorite sci-fi theme.

Pisces (February 19 to March 20): Pisces, the Fish, likes to get lost in alternate realities. Deeply involving stories or movies, from drama to romance to fairy tales—these are all favorites. Fantasy, from *The Lord of the Rings* to *The Chronicles of Narnia*, captivate the Pisces imagination. Role-playing games or constructing elaborate other worlds is her idea of fun. Seafood is a must (along with a colorful bowl of Swedish gummy fish). And mixing water games with fantasy (mermaids, sea monsters, the lost city of Atlantis) would be heaven.

Sunday in May

Ah, a Sunday in May. I look at Georges Seurat's iconic *A Sunday Afternoon on the Island of La Grande Jatte,* and I can smell the sweet air and feel the vibe of the people enjoying a postwinter airing. This painting looks as casual as a Sunday in May, but it took Seurat nearly two years to complete, a work that was the result of meticulous planning, not casual at all!

Who can play?

Ages 9 and up.

What do we need?

Good-quality paper for sketching or painting, pastels or paints, brushes and accoutrements. Magazines, scissors, glue. Sound track to Stephen Sondheim's *Sunday in the Park*. Equipment to listen.

Running time?

An hour or two.

Budget?

$$

What's the Palooza?

Take a good, close look at Georges Seurat's master-piece and create a simple work using the pointil-list technique. Seurat's painting, unofficially known as *Sunday in the Park,* is made up of more than three million dots of paint on the canvas. What was the point of pointillism? It was all about the scientific rela-tionship between color and light. He had been studying color theory (see Goethe, p. 210), that spots of primary colors could beneficially blend together, seen from the right distance. He also played with the idea that side-by-side dashes of paint might add vibrancy to the image that couldn't be achieved with ordinary extended brushstrokes.

First, check out Seurat's masterpiece at the Art Institute of Chicago at www.artic.edu/artaccess/AA_Impression ist/pages/IMP_7.shtml. Use the close-up feature to zoom in on details in the painting. Another terrific resource is *Seurat and the Making of "La Grande Jatte,"* the catalog of a major exhibition of the same name at the Chicago Art Institute. This book tells the story of how Seurat created his masterpiece and offers many close-ups of the can-vas, showing precisely what combination of colors and brushstrokes Seurat used. These are the elements you will work with to create your own pointillist piece—

color combinations, length of brushstroke, and direction of brushstroke.

Now choose a subject of your own and get painting. You don't need to paint an elaborate scene like Seurat to experiment with the pointillist style. A simple vase with flowers or a bowl of apples or a portrait will work just as well. Or take a familiar image (a soda can, a jar of peanut butter). Play with the color combinations as you paint; what happens when you add a tiny dash of red between larger bits of green? Step back from time to time as you work to observe the technique's overall effect. You might even try to paint one version of your subject using regular broad strokes and one using pointillism, to compare the outcome.

pointillism, n.: The technique of applying small strokes or dots of color to a surface so that from a distance, they blend together.

Painter or Composer?

It wasn't just the pointillist painting technique that distinguished Seurat and *La Grande Jatte*. Seurat was an intense student of composition, obsessed with finding just the right combination of figures and features to carefully arrange in his painting. Over the course of the two years it took to complete the painting, Seurat painted dozens of smaller studies that focused on individual details he was considering including in his larger painting. In this way, he collected the more than forty characters he intended to use in *La Grande Jatte* and practiced what form they would take and where they would be positioned in the painting. For instance, one early study featured the model for what would ultimately be the little girl in white who is at the center of *La Grande Jatte*. In this study, the little girl is walking alone in the top right-hand corner of the scene. In the final painting, she walks alongside a lady in a rose-colored skirt, a figure he'd also developed on her own in a separate study.

In preparation for his work on the final canvas, Seurat created sev-

eral compositional studies, where he tested the arrangement of his intended figures, trying them first this way, then that, until he was happy with their placement. He also noodled with details like where the shadows and light would fall, or whether a character was standing, sitting, or engaged in an activity. The dogs and boats in the scene are carefully placed—and that monkey on a leash in the foreground is no accident!

To play with the idea of composition, go through a variety of magazines and cut out images of all different kinds of figures and objects—people doing different things and wearing different kinds of clothing, grown-ups, children, animals, and objects like trees, a suitcase, a streetlight, or a stop sign. The more variety, the better. Now arrange them on your paper canvas, testing them in different spots, developing interesting relationships between the figures and objects. You can coax a little humor out of your scene by putting unlikely figures together—a basketball star crossing the street with an elderly lady, a policeman talking to a poodle.

Use your contemporary cutout figures to create your own version of *La Grande Jatte*. What would your group look like on a Sunday afternoon in Central Park? Or create a similarly elaborate scene but with a different theme. How about a modern scene crowded with children playing different sports and games, à la Pieter Brueghel's *Children's Games?* When you've got a composition you like, glue the figures to the paper. Like Seurat's, your picture can be a work in progress. Add details you find later in magazines or newspapers; Seurat added a cigar to the hand of one figure long after his painting was "finished." (Can you spot the cigar when you look at *La Grande Jatte?*)

Sondheim's Sunday

Composer Stephen Sondheim was so inspired by *La Grande Jatte,* he wrote a Pulitzer Prize–winning Broadway musical about it: *Sunday in the Park with George*. His story brings the characters of the painting to life, and throws the artist himself in the mix as well. The main characters are George, an artist, and his sweetie, Dot. George is creating a painting not unlike *La Grande Jatte*, but from a scene by the river that is not quite so, well, perfect as Seurat's. In George's live setting, the human subjects are rowdy and loud, and Dot, who George is using as one of his subjects, is fidgeting and complaining. George figures out that with a few million strokes of his paintbrush, he can turn troublesome young boys into angels and fidgety Dot into the picture of serenity. Eventually, all the imperfect live characters become cleaned and polished on the canvas, as George manages to construct a scene of perfect balance, order, and loveliness. Unfortunately, George became so preoccupied with perfecting his painting, he lost track of his relationship with Dot, who has decided to leave him. The story fast-forwards a couple of generations to a scene with a modern artist (who also happens to be George's grandson) struggling with his own creativity.

Sondheim managed to translate his affection for *La Grande Jatte*, the painting, and turn it into a lively theatrical exploration of what is art—something perfect or something real? The production is filled with color, both visual and musical (take note of the "dots" of sound that echo Seurat's pointillistic style of painting). Listen to the original cast recording of *Sunday in the Park with George*, featuring Mandy Patinkin and Bernadette Peters. Or watch the terrific video or DVD of the live-audience performance, also featuring Patinkin and Peters.

june
paloozas

Deep Blue Sea

When Jacques Cousteau brought the ocean into our living rooms with *The Undersea World of Jacques Cousteau* in 1966, it was as if he'd pulled back the curtain on a beautiful mystery. Sure, now we have entire cable channels devoted to nature and earth science, but back then, it was all deep blue and brand-new. He's one of my all-time heroes.

Who can play?
Ages 6 and up.

What do we need?
Snorkel and mask, notebook, pen or pencil, colored pencils, lidded plastic containers for specimen collection, field guide to seashells and coastal fish and animals, disposable underwater camera.

Running time?
An afternoon at the beach, a week, or a lifetime.

Budget?
$$

What's the Palooza?

Jacques Cousteau was a true *mousquemer*—a musketeer of the sea. Instantly recognizable in his signature red seaman's cap, he was a fearless, boundless, swashbuckling undersea explorer, whose love of the ocean and her mysteries was contagious. He could never learn enough about what was going on "down there" and was passionate about sharing his adventures and discoveries with people who would otherwise never see it for themselves.

Mousquemer—Moi?

In the manner of Jacques Cousteau, become a musketeer of the sea. You don't have to go out on the high seas—just make your way to the beach, put on a mask and snorkel, and do some shoreside exploring. Who knows? If you start your snooping at the edge of the sea, the beauty and mysteries of the ocean deep may lure you to a lifetime of exploring, the way it did for Jacques Cousteau.

Start by wading out a bit to a spot where the water is clear and the surf is calm, put on your goggles and snorkle, and take a look at what's in the water. You may see schools of tiny fish darting around your legs or crabs creeping on the surface of the sand. Notice the different types of seaweed floating on the surface of the water and below. Some kinds are big and rubbery, others more feathery and light. If you have a waterproof disposable camera and the water is clear enough, take pictures of the plants and creatures you see.

When the tide goes out, look closely at what's going on in the calm, shallow tide pools it leaves behind. (Ask the lifeguards where the good tide pools are.) There are loads of plants and animals that live in these pools—hermit crabs, limpets and barnacles, mussels, starfish, snails, sea urchins, and sand dollars. The areas around big rocks and jetties are usually busy with sea life. When you find an area with lots of critters, observe the activity for a while. Watch for patterns of behavior—does the hermit crab scoot back and forth between two rocks, looking for food? Does he work alone or with his buddies? Is there any interaction between different critters? On the way back to your beach blanket, look for air holes where crabs and clams have dug into the wet sand at the edge of the water. Use a small rake to rake up the dirt and see if you can find the creature under the wet sand.

Jacques Cousteau was born on June 11, 1910.

Tidemark Detective

Don't limit your explorations to things under the water. When the tide reaches its highest point on the beach and then starts to recede, it leaves a line of sea debris on the sand called a tidemark. The tidemark reveals many secrets of what's in the ocean, from shells and seaweed to fish bones and mermaid's purses (shark's egg cases). Take a stick and poke through the tidemark. Collect specimens in plastic containers and use a good field guide to seashells and sea life to identify what you find. Mark the date and location

you found each item on the container. Other fun stuff to collect from the tidemark might be driftwood, sea glass, and lovely smooth stones. Make a sea sculpture with your beach booty.

Water Log

Keep a notebook log of the things you find at the beach. Make notes about any sea creatures you find, as well as any plants you come across in the water or the beach. Write down where and when you discovered it, and a description of what you saw; include a small drawing to help you remember what it looked like. Like Jacques

The Lady *Calypso*

The most famous ship used in Jacques Cousteau's explorations and adventures was the *Calypso*. The *Calypso* was originally a Royal Navy minesweeper, turned ferry when Cousteau found her in Malta. The ship was made over into an oceanographic ship and launched on its first expedition, to the Red Sea, in 1951. The *Calypso* was outfitted with a special underwater observation compartment, with eight portholes so the crew could actually watch the undersea world go by as they were under sail. The world came to know *Calypso* well through her regular appearances in Cousteau's film documentaries and television shows.

Calypso made some thirty voyages over forty years with Cousteau and his crews, but was sadly damaged beyond repair when she was hit by a barge in the port of Singapore in 1996. Today, the ship *Alcyone* has taken over for the *Calypso* in further explorations. In the future, the *Calypso II* will be launched as an environmental observatory that will enable future expeditions to be followed in real time via the Internet. Visit the Cousteau Society Web site at www.cousteau.org to view pictures and plans of these famous boats, and see just where they've taken ocean explorers over the years.

Cousteau, take underwater photos of what you see. This may also be the only way to record the tidemark specimens you collect—they may be too smelly to take home in the car. See how many different things you can find in one trip to the beach, over an entire summer, or throughout your lifetime. Highlights would include, of course, whale or dolphin or sea turtle sightings. But you may also become such an ocean connoisseur that your best find is a rare form of plankton. Imagine what Cousteau's notebooks must have contained!

Shore Report

In his later years, Jacques Cousteau became the voice of environmentalism throughout the world, traveling the globe trying to teach the planet to save itself. For all of his inventions and amazing adventures, he considered his efforts to save Alaska, the Antarctic, and the Amazon his most important lifelong contribution.

Don't wait until someone tells *you* there's a problem with the environment—pay attention to it for yourself. When you're making your ocean explorations, look for

Good Sea Scoop

Peterson First Guide to Shells and *Peterson First Guide to Seashores* are great introductory field guides for your seaside exploration. Check out *The Living Sea*, by Jacques Cousteau; it's a wonderfully enthusiastic and personal account of some of the milestones of underwater exploration and invention, as well as a tour of the world's oceans. Also look for the book Cousteau wrote with his son, Philippe, called *The Shark: Splendid Savage of the Sea*. Most of Cousteau's film and television documentaries (he made more than one hundred of them) are difficult to find, but you should rent any episodes of *The Undersea World of Jacques Cousteau* that you can get your hands on.

The Seven Seas

The phrase *the Seven Seas* doesn't just describe seven seas. It's kind of an all-encompassing term that refers to all the oceans and seas of the world. Look for these on a map or globe, and daydream about exploring them all one day!

Arctic Ocean
Atlantic Ocean
Pacific Ocean
Indian Ocean
Southern Ocean*
Mediterranean Sea
Caribbean Sea
South China Sea
Bering Sea
East China Sea
Japan Sea
Andaman Sea
North Sea
Red Sea
Baltic Sea
Caspian Sea
Black Sea
Aral Sea
Sea of Galilee
Gulf of Mexico
Persian Gulf

* In 2000, the Hydrographic Organization gave a name to a fifth world ocean, the Southern Ocean, which is made up of southern portions of the Atlantic, Indian, and Pacific Oceans.

Language of the Ocean

Abyss
Atoll
Basalt
Conchology
Continental shelf
Delta
Echolocation
Estuary
Floe
Frond
Gill slits
Guyot
Hydrophone
Ichthyology
Intertidal zone
Kelp
Krill
Lagoon
Nekton
Plankton
Rift
Sediment
Tentacle
Thermocline
Zooplankton

signs of damage to the underwater wildlife or coastline. Pollution from people, ships, and factories in the form of litter, fuel, chemicals, and waste will eventually take their toll on shore life. Garbage and litter is easy to spot. But damage from causes you can't see, like chemicals from faraway factories, you need to look closely for. Has an area that should be thriving with plants, fish, and other sea animals turned into an undersea ghost town? Is there ugly goo in the tidemark that may indicate a chemical or oil spill? If you have questions or concerns about what you see, call the local town hall and ask to speak to the person in charge of environmental matters. Your observations may help clue others in to an important problem.

Stars and Stripes

I knew a young girl (she's now a grown woman) who used to celebrate Flag Day every year by affixing a small flag to the arm of a lawn chair, where she'd quietly sit all afternoon in her front yard, taking honks and waves from passersby who appreciated her tender little patriotic streak. I like to think of Flag Day as a chance to give Old Glory an affectionate hug.

What's the Palooza?

On June 14, 1777, the Second Continental Congress passed the Flag Resolution, which resolved "that the flag of the United States be thirteen stripes, alternate red and white; that the union be thirteen stars, white in a blue field representing a new constellation." Then they adopted the flag designed by an upholsterer that General George Washington knew, whose name was Betsy Ross.

It seems that in May of 1776, a secret committee including Washington visited Betsy Ross to talk to her about making a flag representing the thirteen colonies about to declare their independence from England. George Washington already had ideas for the flag, one of which included using six-point stars. Betsy Ross politely disagreed, and proceeded to precisely fold a piece of paper, which she snipped only once with her scissors to produce a perfectly proportioned five-point star. With that bit of showmanship, Betsy was awarded the commission—and free license to use the five-pointed

---

Who can play?
All ages.

What do we need?
Scratch paper, poster paper, colored construction paper, crayons, markers, paint, craft sponges, miscellaneous crafty bric-a-brac, scissors, glue, fabric scraps, needle, and thread.

Running time?
One to two hours.

Budget?
$

star. Her ultimate design of thirteen stars arranged in a circle is what is now called the "Betsy Ross Flag."

Be Betsy

What if you were Betsy Ross, and George Washington asked you to design the first flag of the United States? Take the details from the resolution and design your own flag. How wide will the stripes be? Will they be horizontal or vertical? How will you arrange the thirteen white stars "on a blue field"? What kind of stars would they be—George's six-pointers or Betsy's fives? Try out a few different ideas and sketch them on a piece of paper. Pick your best design and make your new "first" U.S.

Flag Etiquette

- - - - - - -

There are special ways to treat the American flag—rules to follow to show respect to one of our most prized national symbols, and to all those that gave their lives defending it. Here are some basics:

The flag is usually flown from sunrise to sunset. It should not be flown at night without a light on it.

The flag should not be flown in rainy or stormy weather.

After a national tragedy or death, the flag is flown at half staff (on land) or half mast (on a ship)—either for thirty days or for other lengths of time, by presidential proclamation.

When flown on the same pole as other flags, the American flag is always flown at the top of the pole. State flags and other flags fly below it.

The union (the blue field with the stars) is always on top. The only exception to this is that a ship may fly the flag upside down to indicate the vessel is in distress.

The flag should never touch the ground.

The flag should be folded flat, not rolled or bunched up, for storage.

Old, tattered flags may be burned or buried, but should never be thrown out like regular trash. Many veterans groups hold official flag disposal ceremonies if you need to get rid of an old flag.

flag out of colored construction paper, or colored or painted on posterboard. Dip a star-shaped sponge in paint to make the stars of your flag. Or use the star-shaped sponge and a roller sponge to make stripes with fabric paint on an old pillowcase. Create a patriot's gallery of your designs.

Betsy's Star Magic

Go to www.ushistory.org/ betsy/ flagstar.html to learn the secret to making Betsy Ross's five-pointed star. It may be simple, but it sure wowed old George Washington.

The Newfangled Flag

Examine the U.S. flag as it is today. As each state joined the union, the flag was redesigned to accommodate another star. With each revision, the aim was to sneak in one or two more stars while trying to keep the same basic design. Over the years, the blue filled in with more and smaller stars, but each new star was successfully added to the design until we reached our current flag of fifty stars and thirteen stripes.

Design a brand-new current flag. Forget the traditional stars and stripes. What if the stars were arranged in a spiral—like a snail shell? How about in concentric circles? Why not diamond shapes or triangles? Think of how you would represent the country of fifty states we are today. Stick with the red, white, and blue color scheme, and the need for fifty of one thing and thirteen of another, and create an entirely new flag scheme. Attach your flag to a stick or pole or hang it in your window.

Our Family, Our Flag

Every country has its own flag. Just like the American flag, each country chooses the colors and symbols it displays to reflect things that are important to it. Take a look at other countries' flags and try to figure out what they mean. For instance, the flag of the former USSR shows a hammer, a sickle, and a star. What do you think they meant to

Vexillology, n.:
The study of flags.

represent with those symbols? The maple leaf on the Canadian flag is another striking symbol, as is the sliver moon and star on the flag of Turkey. Check out www.flagspot.net/flags/ for a glimpse of the many different flags that fly around the world.

Use the different colors and symbols of the flags around the world as inspiration to create your own family flag. Write down some ideas about things that are important in your family. Choose the colors and symbols that would best represent your family. If your family enjoys the outdoors or is committed to the environment, perhaps your flag features a tree. What if you're animal lovers or sports fiends or bookworms? How would you represent these on a family flag? Perhaps you want to convey important ideals or values your family shares, like justice or fairness or compassion. What symbols—objects or animals, maybe—might you incorporate? What colors would you use to express these ideas? Once you've created a family flag, you've got a symbol of what makes you who you are. Make note cards or placemats or T-shirts that wave your flag for you.

Sing a Flag Song

It is said that it was the heroic defense of Fort McHenry against British attack on Baltimore during the War of 1812 that inspired a young lawyer named Francis Scott Key to write "The Star-Spangled Banner." This became the granddaddy of flag songs, of course, but there are plenty more worth belting out Broadway-style on a day like Flag Day. George M. Cohan's "You're a Grand Old Flag" comes to mind, as does John Philip Sousa's "Stars and Stripes Forever" and Becket and Shaw's "Columbia, the Gem of the Ocean," to name a couple of old-timey favorites. And search out Johnny Cash's "Ragged Old Flag" and Randy Newman's "Follow the Flag Forever" for contemporary flag-hugging songs to sing on Flag Day.

Our flag is our national ensign, pure and simple, behold it! Listen to it! Every star has a tongue and every stripe is articulate

—Senator Robert C. Winthrop of Massachusetts (1809–1894)

Pops!

What sings of summer like lying in a hammock, slurping a Popsicle? Nothing I can think of!

What's the Palooza?

Just about any kind of Popsicle is all right with me, but how about making your own, in the mouthwatering Mexican style? These frozen treats are called *paletas*, or "little shovels," and are a local specialty in the village of Tocumbo, in the Mexican state of Michoacan. The story goes that two cousins from the village opened a tiny shop in Mexico City in the late 1940s and had tremendous success selling their icy sweet treats. Many other villagers followed suit, and eventually all of Mexico was dotted with *paleterias*. Now you can find *paleterias* in the United States, from Texas to California and New Mexico to New York.

Paletas are famous for their creative combinations of fresh ingredients. These pops can be creamy (*paletas de leche),* made with milk (or cream or yogurt) and sweet tropical fruits and berries, or they can be water-based *(paletas de agua),* made of just fruit and juice or sugar. Sometimes the fruit and other ingredients are pureed to a smooth consistency before freezing, and sometimes the fruit is left a little chunky. There are as many flavors as there are possible combinations of ingredients, all of them as tasty as a summer day.

Make Your Own

The basic recipe for a *paleta* is simple and infinitely adaptable, according to the kind of fruit(s) and other ingredients you decide to use. You can make it with one kind of fruit—mango with a twist of lime juice is a classic. Or you can make it with a combination of fruits—strawberries and bananas, pineapple and orange, or three kinds of melon, to name a few. You can puree all the fruits together or puree each individually and add them to your pop molds separately to create a layered effect.

In a blender or food processor, combine:

2–3 cups of fruit, cut into 1-inch chunks if necessary
2–6 tablespoons of sugar, depending on the natural
    sweetness of the fruit and your taste
Fresh orange, lemon, or lime juice, by the tablespoon,
    to taste (optional)
1 cup of milk or yogurt, if making a *paleta de leche*

Pour the puree into six small plastic cups. Cover with plastic wrap and put in the freezer until they begin to set, about 90 minutes. Insert Popsicle or lollipop sticks with 2 inches showing and return to the freezer until completely frozen, at least another 90 minutes. When you're ready to eat, run the cup under warm water until the *paleta* pops out. Then get lickin'!

Paleta Suprema

Experiment with flavor combinations until you come up with one or two blue-ribbon winners that will be your signature pops, the ones you'll become famous for! Think about different fruit pairings and whether the paleta would be better *de leche* or just icy. Are there any other kinds of ingredients you might add that would snazz up your pop? Play around with raisins, citrus zest, shredded coconut, mini-marshmallows, gummy bears— even herbs like mint. Would a splash of tonic water or ginger ale give your *paleta* some pop? When you hit a home run on a recipe, you'll know it—your taste-testers will be begging for more! Use these sample combos as inspiration to invent your own:

Please Pass the Rambutan

You don't have to settle for the same-old, same-old fruit you find in your local grocery store chains. Visit farmstands, greenmarkets, ethnic groceries, and online fruit sources such as www.manhattanfruitier.com/exotic/exoticfruit.html to find wonderful varieties of familiar and exotic fruits from around the world. Get fluent in fruit and become a fruit connoisseur! A real *paleterissimo*!

Exotic and Tropical Fruit
Asian pear
Atemoya
Avocado
Banana
Carambola
Cherimoya
Feijoa
Guava
Kiwi
Ladyfinger banana
Longan
Lychee
Mango
Mangosteen
Papaya
Passion fruit
Pineapple
Plantain
Pomegranate
Rambutan
Starfruit
Tamarind

Mediterranean Fruits
Cactus pear
Carob
Fig
Loquat
Olive
Persimmon
Pistachio

Berries
Blackberry
Blackcurrant
Blueberry
Boysenberry
Cranberry
Gooseberry
Loganberry
Marionberry
Ollalieberry
Black raspberry
Red raspberry
Salmonberry
Strawberry

Citrus Fruits
Blood orange
Clementine
Citron
Key lime
Kumquat
Lemon
Lime
Limequat
Mandarin orange
Minneola tangelo
Navel orange
Pummelo
Red grapefruit
Satsuma
Seville orange
Tangerine
Ugli fruit
Valencia orange

Grapes
Beauty seedless
Black Corinth
Cardinal
Champagne
Concord
Emperor
Muscat
Perlette
Red flame
Red globe
Ribier
Thompson seedless
Tokay

Pomes
Braeburn apple
Cortland apple
Fuji apple
Gala apple
Golden Delicious
  apple
Granny Smith apple
Gravenstein apple
Jonathan apple
McIntosh apple
Newton Pippin
  apple
Northern Spy apple
Red Delicious apple
Rome Beauty apple
Winesap apple
Bartlett pear
Bosc pear
Comice pear
D'Anjou pear
Red Bartlett pear
Seckel pear
Winter Nellis pear
Quince

Mandarin orange/vanilla yogurt
Cantaloupe and orange/honeydew melon and lime/
    a hint of minced fresh mint
Blueberry/custardy lemon yogurt
Pineapple/coconut/cream
Kiwi/honeydew melon

Use unusual molds to make your pops distinctive. Little Dixie cups always work well, of course, but you can also make your pops in small tart tins for a fancy look or in pointy water-cooler cups for a space-age pop. Cut the bottoms out of an egg carton as a stand for your pointy pops as they set in the freezer. Or use a tray for large ice cubes for a chunky square pop.

Name your creation: Blue Banana Bonanza. The Mighty Melon Monster. Papaya at Sunset. Get fancy and use the Spanish words for the fruit—*Piña Plátano con Frambuesa* (Pineapple/Banana with Raspberry).

Paleteria!

Pretend you're one of those two cousins going to Mexico City to open up the first *paleteria.* What's the name of your shop? Petey's Paletas? Izzy's Ice Castle? I know—Paletapalooza! Create a logo for your *paleteria* and copy it onto blank mailing-label-style stickers. Settle on your six best *paletas* (a couple of *de leches,* a few *aguas*) and give them great names. Make a bunch of each flavor and create wrappers for them (wax or plastic bags decorated with your logo stickers). Wrap a large cooler in butcher paper and decorate it with your logo. Make a sign listing your *paletas,* fill the cooler with ice and *paletas,* load it all into a wagon, and you've got a pushcart *paleteria!* Set up shop at a Little League game or a neighborhood gathering, and you'll put the lemonade stands out of business.

blow this Popsicle stand, v. phrase, idiom: Clear out, move on, get out of town.

The first day of summer is between June 20 and June 23, depending on the moment the earth's axis points at the sun.

Off the Charts

Invent some *paletas* that go beyond the fruit/sugar/milk spectrum. Maybe something savory or spicy. How about pumpkin, milk, and cinnamon? Or rice pudding and raisins? Avocado and lime? Here's a great favorite at many authentic *paleterias: pepino con chile,* a surprisingly refreshing combination of cucumber, watermelon, lime juice, and a pinch of chile powder. Use anything that's in season any time of the year. Think of the fruit and vegetable stand—and your cupboard and spice rack—as a palette of flavors and colors you can choose from to create one-of-a-kind *paletas.*

Superdude

What kid doesn't dream about being superhuman, dazzling one and all with supersized powers of speed, agility, strength, or heightened sensory perception? But what about the lesser-known powers, such as the mindbending ability to find loose change in the depths of the family car? Or the jaw-dropping aptitude for reading words backward? How about an undiscovered gift for speed-bagging groceries? Ordinary activities turn into extraordinary undertakings by the superdudes in your house.

What's the Palooza?

Become your own superhero by designing a cool costume to match your special powers. Great at doing dishes? Turn into Dish Man, armed with rubber gloves and a spray bottle to defend the universe from dirty cups and glasses. Can you draw a crowd with your bubblegum-blowing skills? Transform yourself into Bubble Kid, pack your pockets with the gum of your choice, and snap your bubbles to scare away intruders.

What's Your Story?

Flesh out your alter ego by inventing the story of how your superhero came to be. Invent a planet where your superhero came from or an explanation of how your superhero came upon his powers, such as Peter Parker's radioactive spider bite or Dr. David Banner's gamma radiation exposure. With a notebook, markers, and a superstrong imagination, create a comic-book tale of how your superhero came to be.

Who can play?
Ages 3 to 6.

What do we need?
An old pillowcase or fabric for a cape, felt or fabric paint or markers for lettering, sunglasses, boots, gloves, or other accessories of your own design.

Running time?
A couple of hours.

Budget?
$

Superman's birthday is June 30.

The Buddy System

Batman had Robin, Green Arrow had Speedy, Captain America had Bucky, and Power Man had Iron Fist. These famous sidekicks joined their superhero in crime-fighting capers and other exotic endeavors. Create a sidekick to go with your alter ego superhero. Dish Man can have Dry Guy, and Peanut Butter Pal can join Bubble Kid to unstick the hero from certain sticky situations. Develop a special sidekick persona and add him to your comic book adventures, complete with a story of his own.

Signature Superhero Sayings

"To the bat cave, Robin!" —Batman

"Truth, justice, and the American way!" —Superman

"Spider senses tingling!" —Spiderman

"Pussy willows galore!" —Catwoman

"I speak loudly for those who have no voice." —Captain America

"Hulk smash, Hulk destroy." —the Incredible Hulk

Superhero Science

The classic superhero superstrengths have some very scientific reasoning behind them. As Spiderman, Peter Parker developed the ability to make webs, stick to surfaces, and sense when danger was near. But Spidey was really mimicking the power that ordinary spiders already have. They are superlative spinners of silken webs that, based on a ratio of weight, have twice the strength as steel.

Diana Prince's Wonder Woman wielded a lie-detecting lasso. The creators of this comic book hero were also behind the invention of the lie detector, or polygraph, which can determine fluctuating signs like heart rate, blood pressure, and respiratory rate that a person may show while eluding the truth. While the lie detector can't identify an actual lie, it can measure differences in behavior and body functions during an exam.

The creators of the Incredible Hulk were inspired by seeing a woman lifting the rear end of a car to rescue her trapped child. In the comic book series, David Banner is exposed to gamma radiation and transforms, when he's angry, into a man of extraordinary strength. It's true that at times of great stress, hormones are released into the human body that increase blood flow and oxygen and make unusual feats of strength possible.

Archenemy Number 1

Every superhero in history has a nemesis, someone who consistently gets in the way of Doing Good. Lex Luthor plagued Superman, and Spiderman was constantly hounded by the Green Goblin. Invent an archenemy that battles with your superhero, create a situation where your superhero must match wits with this evil character, and include the tale in your comic-book story line.

Good Books

Read all of Dav Pilkey's *Captain Underpants* titles to get ideas for a comical superhero. Check out Wendelin Van Draanen's *Shredderman* books, too. And get lost in *The Official Handbook of the Marvel Universe* for loads of inspiration.

Make It a Party!

Invites: Decorate your invitation with a drawing of an original superhero or superhero logos. "Fly! Leap! Teleport! to Jennifer's Superhero Birthday Party. Bring your secret powers!"

Food and Decor: Cutouts of planets, aluminum-foil lightning bolts, plastic lab beakers. Serve energy drinks, footlong submarine sandwiches, giant Twizzlers, and superhero cupcakes topped with action figures.

Activities: Superhero Olympics, with bubble-blowing, backward-running, and dish-doing contests. Pick activities according to the special powers of the guest superheroes, or try an obstacle course, relay races, and a scavenger hunt that capitalizes on these. Play blindfolded games such as taste-testing and smelling, which call for sense sensitivity.

Favors: Comic books, plastic action figures, rubber superballs, flashlights, and plain plastic eyeglasses (to shield true identity, of course).

july
paloozas

T.I.B.

Fireworks are always great fun, and I never turn down a Fourth of July barbecue. But from time to time over the years, I have found it helpful to take a moment on this day to remind myself of what we're shooting off the screamers and bottle rockets about. This is a palooza for the whole family.

What's the Palooza?

In the early 1950s, the distinguished broadcast journalist Edward R. Murrow's radio show, *This I Believe,* was the most-listened-to radio program in the world. Curious to understand how a country that had survived World War II and now looked into a hopeful future would describe itself, Murrow invited men and women from all walks of life to say out loud what they believed in. As Mr. Murrow said, "The only way of discovering what people believe is to ask them."

When you consider that all those Revolutionary War heroes and patriots fought for American independence so that we could be free to believe what we want to believe, it's kind of funny that very few people are able to express what they believe. As you enjoy your day of red, white, and blue celebration, think about how you would put into words what you think is true and important. Then create your own T.I.B (This I Believe). It can be whatever mixed bag of ideas make up your personal philosophy. A friend of mine's is short and sweet, and a little bit funny:

I believe in the whole truth (not half truths), the whole person (not just what he looks like), and whole milk (not skim). Anything in its entirety deserves my full appreciation.

Make a list of things that matter to you—your family or friends, your home, your pets, your baseball glove. What is it about your family that you like so much? What qualities do you appreciate about them? Their loyalty to each other? The fact that they're always there when you need them? Or maybe it's their loopy sense of humor. These are the things you believe are important about your family. What about other things? Your dog? That's easy—you love him for his sweet nature and endlessly wagging tail. Do you believe in your dog? No! But you do believe it's important to have someone who's always there to show you devotion, no matter what. You love your baseball glove for its worn leather, ripe smell, and the time you caught the game-winning out with it in the Little League championship. What might that add up to on your T.I.B? "I believe in little moments of heroism that make me feel I've done my best."

Now write up your personal philosophy as a T.I.B. You can organize it in a straightforward list format: "I believe in close, honest friendships. I believe in clear, star-filled skies. I believe in holding hands during scary movies. . . ." Or you can write it free-form, like an essay that paints a rounded picture of the things you think are important. Sometimes a simple statement is all it takes. Modern dance legend Martha Graham declared:

I am a dancer. I believe that we learn by practice. Whether it means to learn to dance by practicing dancing or to learn to live by practicing living, the principles are the same.

You can also tell a story that illustrates what you believe. One contributor to Mr. Murrow's radio program, a scientist, told of a "long, lonesome winter" he spent living with an Eskimo family, when he learned from them "when to think, when to eat, when to play, when to be joyful, in just amount." His time with them living in a hut and eating seal meat enabled him to identify exactly what he believed in: "The brotherhood of man, the virtue of patience, the need of self-evaluation, the unity of family, and the method of science."

Once you've written your T.I.B., you can illustrate it

To be persuasive, we must be believable; to be believable we must be credible; to be credible, we must be truthful.

—Edward R. Murrow
(1908–1965)

with drawings or family photographs or images clipped from magazines and collaged around the edges of your T.I.B. Save it and look at it from time to time to remind yourself of who you are. Make changes as you think of new, true things. And pop a firecracker of gratitude that we live in a place where we each can march to our own drummer and believe what we want to.

The Family Creed

Create a family T.I.B, a creed that states your team philosophy. It can be short—Work hard, play hard, get enough sleep. Or it can be longer and more encompassing. One family I know has posted their T.I.B. (entitled "Our Family Rules") on the side of the fridge for years:

1. We choose and use our words carefully. We speak kindly, gently, intelligently, and truthfully.

2. We do not screech or raise our voices, mimic others unkindly, or use sharp, hurtful words.

3. We share responsibility for the care of each other, our pets, and our home.

4. We respect each other's time, work, and property.

5. We hug and show love and comfort for each other, each and every day, because it feels good and because we need it.

Just Ask

Edward Murrow managed to convince hundreds of ordinary people—homemakers, soldiers, businesspeople—as well as famous writers, artists, scientists, and politicians, to try to express what they believed. Among them were composer Leonard Bernstein, statesman Dag Hammarskjold, actress Helen Hayes, writer Aldous Huxley, poet Carl Sandburg, and even President Harry Truman. How did he get a U.S. president to share his personal philosophy with an audience of millions of listeners? He just asked.

Ask people you know if they are able to say out loud what they believe in. Challenge them to write a T.I.B. of their own. You already know from your own experience that it's easy to suggest but a little trickier to do. You might be able to get them to summarize their life philosophy bumper-sticker-style.

Street Games

When I was a kid, a huge oak tree was cut down in our neighborhood and left in big chunks on the ground for more than a year. It didn't take long for us to invent a game for those logs; we called it Leaping Logs, and it was a twist on tag that involved jumping from log to log. Kids can turn *anything* into a game. This palooza celebrates some of the all-time great games that were created by kids making the most of the quirks of their home and neighborhood.

Who can play?
Ages 6 and up.

What do we need?
Bottle caps and sidewalk chalk; a sturdy dowel-like stick, about three feet long; and a Spaldeen.

Running time?
An afternoon.

Budget?
Free or $

What's the Palooza?

You know the nooks and crannies of your neighborhood better than anyone else. Invent your own game that is unique to the architecture and the shapes of your street or yard. With the basic equipment of balls, sticks, bottle caps, and chalk, and features like stoops, curbs, or walls, you can make your sidewalk, street, or driveway into a giant game board. The beauty of the classic street games described below is that every bunch of kids who has ever played them invented their own versions. Now think of ways to make them your own.

Skully

This city street game will remind you a little bit of a mix of marbles and hopscotch, but it involves throwing skully caps (bottle caps or similar disks) across a blacktop board that's about seven feet square, marked with numbers 1 through 13 (as indicated on the illustration).

You can also mark out your board on the floor of a basement, garage, or wherever you have room, using painter's masking tape so you don't harm the floor. The "skull" of the game's name refers to the boxes at the center of the game, which can act as a trap as you try to advance through the game.

The object of the game is to shoot your cap from the starting line to the 1 box, then on to each numbered square through 13, then work your way back to the 1 box. It'll take a little practice to get this shooting/flicking action down. After a player has completed his first 1-to-13-to-1 course, he becomes a "killer," trying to eliminate the other players from the game. A player's turn continues for as long as he continues to land successfully in the next box. Once you get beyond the 1 box, if you hit another player's cap in a box, you're awarded a free extra box. If you hit two (or more) caps in a turn, you get two (or more) extra boxes. Needless to say, this is a favorite strategy for advancing in the game.

Anyone whose cap lands in one of the trapezoid boxes that surround the 13 box in the skull is trapped there until another player hits him or her out, or after losing three turns. The player who hits the "stuck" player gets a bonus of the number of the trapezoid box in which he is stuck. So say you're in the 4 box, going for 5, and you hit out a player in the 6 trapezoid box. This entitles you to advance 6 boxes to the 10 box, ready to go for 11s.

Once you've completed the circuit and become a "killer," your goal is to eliminate the other players. If you're pursuing nonkillers, you have to hit them out three times to eliminate them from the game. If you're pursuing a killer, you only have to hit him once. A killer "owns the board," which means he doesn't have to move through the boxes in numerical order anymore; he can use any box from turn to turn in pursuit of his prey. A nonkiller can become a killer by hitting a killer's cap, which increases the feverish competition until the game's end. The last remaining killer in the game wins.

You can reinvent skully with your own ideas, using fewer numbers on your board or something besides numbers entirely (letters, colors, objects, and so on), a different shape of board (maybe a spiral or triangle), or different rules for advancing or winning. Skully has

Skully Talk

Just as the Inuit have many words for snow, and sailors have a word for every nook and cranny of a ship, there's a whole vocabulary for skully games. Here are a few of the choicest:

baby stuff: Game options that are believed to weaken the game, such as "holdsies" or "spinsies."

blasting: When a cap is shot with the intent of hitting another cap a large distance. Used to slow the other player's progression in the game, because he usually has to take a bunch of turns to get back on the board.

blastsies: A game where blasting is allowed. The alternative is a "no blastsies" game. To be determined before start of play.

game options: The various rules and styles of play mutually agreed upon before the game begins, such as "no blastsies."

hit: When one cap comes in contact with another. Hits are how players earn advance-a-box bonuses.

holdsies: The practice of holding one's cap against the board to prevent it being blasted by another player. See "baby stuff."

marksies: When a player marks a cap's position on the board so it can temporarily be removed from play. Usually used to avoid cap being run over by a car.

out of town: The distance from the skully board that a killer must take his shots. Usually outside of the ordinary distance required for a decent player to shoot his cap. Distance determined before the start of the game.

pipsies: When a player shoots into the next box in one shot. Pipsies usually get the player a two-box bonus, though this is a game option to be determined before the game.

spinsies: A game option that allows a player to touch his cap in the event it lands spinning on its side.

switchsies: Universally despised game option that allows unlimited cap switching during a game to suit the game situation. Usually involves switching to a heavy cap for blasting, or switching to a smaller cap to avoid being hit.

The Fine Art of Making Skully Caps

Half the fun of playing skully is the ritual of making your skully caps. There's no rule about what a skully cap should be made of, though it is agreed among aficionados that if you can't shoot it properly (i.e., it's too big or too small), you shouldn't play with it. There are great strategies for making your skully cap a master blaster on the skully board. You can use twist-off metal soda tops, Snapple-type metal drink tops, or small metal jar lids. Whatever you use, the real secret to a good skully cap is in the weight of it. Often, the top or lid alone is too light to glide effectively across the board, so real skully fiends melt candle or crayon wax in the cap to give it some heft. Have an adult help you melt wax on the stove or in a microwave. Set your caps on a cookie sheet and pour the melted wax into your cap, careful not to let it splatter, (a) because it's hot, and (b) because it's a little messy. Some tricky skully players even set a penny or a nickel in the bottom of the cap before pouring the wax. Experiment with different tops and weights to see what works best for you.

been around since the 1930s and has been transformed by as many kids as have played the game! Go to www.streetplay.com/skully/ for a fantastic guide to the ins and outs of the game, including some of the elaborate rules skully players have dreamed up over the years. Then add your two cents to the history of skully.

Ring-o-Levio

Cross hide-and-go-seek with tag, add a dash of dodgeball, and you've got ring-o-levio! Divide into two equal teams with any number of players. One team represents the hunters, whose goal is to capture all the members of the other team. The hunters designate the front steps, a park bench, a swing set, the garage door, or any other appropriate site as the hunters' jail. The goal of the hunted is to elude capture and free their jailed comrades.

Hunters usually travel in a pack to capture an individual opponent. The capture is accomplished when a hunter grabs an opponent, shouts, "Ring-o-levio, one, two, three!" and escorts the captive to the designated jail, where he or she is held until released by a teammate. It's bad form to hide out in an impossible-to-find spot for hours on end to avoid capture; to be a true ring-o-levio competitor, you must make frequent, teasing appearances. The boldest acts of ring-o-levio bravery take place during the "jail raids," whether in the form of an organized and covert operation or a solo ambush. Once you've run past the guards and touched the base, yell "Home free!" to release your captured comrades. The game ends either when all the players are captured—which can take hours, even days!—or when it's dinnertime.

Stickball

Stickball is a beloved adaptation of baseball that replaces the bat with a broomstick or mop handle, the ball with a lighter, rubber one referred to as a Spaldeen, and the diamond with the street. Stickball, which is believed to have originated in the late eighteenth century, became a signature game on the streets of New York City in the 1920s and 30s. This all-time classic after-school pickup game is now enjoying a revival: many cities have started stickball leagues organized by age group, from the youngest city slickers to the oldest stickball veterans.

To play, first try this basic pitching variation, known as fungo. It is the most common type of stickball, where the batter pitches for him- or herself. Toss the ball in the air with one hand, while holding the bat in the other. Let the ball bounce once as you get into batting position, then clobber the ball at the top of its bounce. Some flamboyant batters build suspense by waiting until the second or third bounce, teasing the spectators. Fungo uses three to four players per team, and is always played in the street or on an open blacktop.

Determine where your bases are—in the original game, it might be a fire hydrant or manhole cover. Just make sure your bases are in safe spots, and that the area of your entire game is protected from traffic. An out is generally constituted by hitting the ball onto a roof or gutter or down a sewer drain, breaking a window (no kidding!), or missing the ball on one or two tries, though this number varies. Besides that, regular baseball rules usually apply (running the bases and so on). Here's where you adapt the game to your own geography, the number of players you have, or your own particular flavor of rules. If you only have a couple of players or a limited space that makes base-running impossible, make it a home-run derby, with wild rules for scoring. Or play it against a wall on a schoolyard blacktop, the way you would play handball, measuring the hit by how far behind you it goes. Watch out for ricochet!

No matter what kind of stickball you like to play, this trick is the gold standard in stickball showmanship: rather than tossing the ball into the air, roll it up and off the end of the stick, then
whack it after its first bounce.

Le Tour

Every summer, the Tour de France makes me want to hop on my bicycle and pedal like the wind. Of course, I don't have to climb the Alps to win my suburban, three-speed version of the Tour! Here's a family tip of the hat to this century-old competition—and the grit and endurance it takes to win.

Who can play?

Anyone who's able (and allowed!) to ride a bike on a road or bike trail. Approximately ages 9 and up.

What do we need?

Bikes, helmets, maps, a calendar, notebook, and stopwatches. White T-shirts (one per rider) and fabric markers, two additional white T-shirts, and colored T-shirts in yellow and green. Plastic water bottles and Sharpies, sidewalk chalk, waste-baskets, and balls.

Running time?

An hour or so of at least three days, or an afternoon of a single day.

Budget?

$$$

What's the Palooza?

Design a safe, quirky multi-legged bike challenge, modeled (very!) loosely on the Tour de France. The first Tour de France (known familiarly as "Le Tour") was staged as a newspaper publicity stunt in 1903. With the exception of the years during the two world wars, the race has taken place every summer since then, drawing top cyclists from around the world to compete on the grueling 3,500-kilometer course. All together, there are twenty days of individual race segments that are anywhere from 160 kilometers to 210 kilometers long (not counting the shorter time trial distances). And all each day's winner gets is a lousy T-shirt! Seriously, there is probably no more coveted prize in all of sports than the *maillot jaune*, or yellow shirt, that is awarded to the rider with the most points each day. The ultimate winner is the rider with the best combined times and points.

Get ready. Sit down with your family and plan your own Le Tour. Get out a local map and identify bike paths that would be good "stages" of your competition. If you bike on the paths in your area regularly and know the different types of terrain, create stages with different challenges (a speed stretch, a hilly climb, a long distance). You can even make a stage in an empty school parking lot that's an obstacle course or relay.

If each of you is an individual competitor within your family, give each person a T-shirt to decorate with a team name and logo. If you're inviting friends or other families to join your Tour, have each team choose a name and logo and decorate team shirts appropriately. How about the Coneheads, sponsored by the fictional ice cream company called "Lickety Splitz"? Decorate your plastic water bottles with your team name and logo, too.

Also create the winners' jerseys. There are several prizes to be won during the real Tour de France, and there is usually a colored jersey associated with each prize. There's the coveted yellow jersey, the green sprint jersey, and polka-dotted jerseys, to name a few. For our purposes, let's have:

Yellow jersey: For the person who is the overall time leader from stage to stage (this is the person whose combined time is lowest).

Red polka-dot jersey: Draw big red polka dots on a white T-shirt to create the "King of the Mountains" jersey. This is awarded to the rider who is first to the top of the most difficult hill.

The Tour de France takes place over three weeks in July.

What Does It Take?

The world's top cyclists have natural physical characteristics in common that enable them to compete in difficult races like the Tour de France—a slim upper frame, strong legs, a sturdy heart, and large lung capacity. Most successful bicyclists also have a combination of a low resting heart rate and the ability to maintain a high heart rate for extended periods of time. A Tour rider reaches a working heart rate of more than 200 beats a minute many times throughout the race. (The average person *never* reaches that heart rate.)

And what does six-time Tour de France winner Lance Armstrong have that the other riders don't? Sally Jenkins, coauthor with Armstrong of *It's Not about the Bike* and *Every Second Counts,* claims that he's got a larger heart than the rest of us and a resting heart rate of just 40 beats per minute, and his body produces less lactic acid than other people's, which helps it recover more easily from stress. And, according to Jenkins, "Nobody works as hard as he does. It's not just the manual labor, it's the constant search for better technology and training methods, the studying of the Tour route, the examining of all the crucial stretches of road down to the manhole covers." Sounds like he eats his Wheaties *and* does his homework!

Green jersey: For the person who works hardest to keep up on a particularly tough stretch. This is the "Atta boy!" or "Go girl!" prize.

Get set. If you're designing a multi-day Tour, mark a calendar with the various stages you've created. Give everyone who is participating a map marked with the stage courses and instructions for start locations and times. If you have a whole bunch of people participating, you should probably have each team run their speed, distance, and difficulty stages on their own, then have everyone come back together to a single location for a final rally or some fun contests (as below). And choose a time and record keeper for each team. Everyone is on the honor system to report their times accurately for the final accounting.

Go! Each Tour de France team consist of nine members, all working to support the leader in his bid to win for the whole team. The idea is to encourage each other; swing back around to ride alongside someone who's struggling. Take turns going for a sprint time or establishing the pace for a long distance. The race can consist of any combination of stages and prizes you invent, so it can be as competitive or just plain fun as you like. Make it an annual event and see who starts their Tour training earliest in the spring!

Tour Twisters

Put your helmets together and come up with bike challenges and mini-contests to play at your post-Tour party, as tiebreakers, or just for fun. Everyone who plays these games needs to be a good enough bike rider to manage the various tasks. Some of these are easiest to pull off in an empty parking lot.

How about slow biking? Mark off 100 feet with two par-

Tour Terminology

----

attack: To make a sudden attempt to ride ahead of a rider or group of riders.

block: Get in the way or slow down in front of rival riders in order to help a teammate get ahead on a breakaway.

echelon: A diagonal paceline, a modification of the single-file formation to adapt to a crosswind.

field sprint: an exciting sprint for the finish line involving a large group of riders.

force the pace: Increase the speed of the race so that other riders have trouble keeping up.

leadout: A rider who helps a teammate by riding just ahead of him in order to provide a windbreak and open a hole in the pack. This sets up the second rider to make an attempt to win a final sprint.

off the back: When a rider falls behind and can't keep pace with another rider or the group.

off the front: When a rider participates in a breakaway, where one or more riders shoot out ahead of the main group in the race.

paceline: A single-file line of riders who take turns breaking the wind at the front.

peloton: The pack of the fastest riders at the front of a road race.

pull off: To remove oneself from the wind-breaking spot at the front of a group of riders and return to a spot within the group.

pull through: Take the front position in a paceline after someone else has "pulled off" and returned to the group.

time trials: Race events where individuals or small teams are timed for a set distance and route.

allel chalk lines drawn about six inches apart. In this slow race, feet are not allowed to touch the ground. No going backward, sideways, or any way but straight ahead. The person to successfully complete the course in the greatest amount of time wins. Or how about a neighborhood bike scavenger hunt, all the items to be collected without getting off your bike? Or a bike relay, where one person hands off something soft and easy to catch (like a sock wad or beanbag) to a teammate, who then pedals like mad to hand off to the next relay rider? Or create a slalom course using rubber cones.

Going Mobile

"I paint with shapes," said the great twentieth-century sculptor Alexander Calder. His lifelong exploration of the relationship between shapes and movement yielded a brand new art form, now a familiar fixture in a baby's nursery, but utterly avant-garde at the time of its invention.

Alexander Calder was born on July 22, 1898.

What's the Palooza?

Venture into Calder's magnificent world of mobiles. Explore the forms he experimented with on his way to inventing and perfecting the mobile. First go to the Calder Organization's excellent Web site to look at examples of Calder's work in different forms; click on "Calder's Work," then "View work by type," to sample the different forms discussed in this palooza (www.calder.org).

Alexander (or "Sandy," as many called him) first began to explore sculpture by manipulating wire. At the age of twenty-seven, he made his first wire sculpture, shaped like a rooster, which doubled as a sundial (he claimed he didn't own a clock to tell him the time.) Later, he would become known for his fascinating wire portraits, which often portrayed his friends. You can replicate Calder's playful portraits by first making a simple sketch of someone, then, using pieces of aluminum wire, trying to transform your pencil sketch into a wire portrait. Use wire that's not too heavy, so you can bend it, wind it, and shape it accordingly. Cut as many pieces as you need to work into your portrait. The more you work with wire, the more interesting detail you can bring to your portrait; you can make eyeglasses, a beard, spiky hair, and whatever you see on your subject's face, like a smile or the arch of an eyebrow. Check out several of Calder's wire portraits by clicking on "wire sculpture" on the Calder Organization Web site.

Hang It Up

Calder was fascinated by motion, and he was particularly interested in the natural movements of air. He hung his wire portraits on string or wire and discovered that the individual elements of the sculptures came to life with the movement of air. If you ever see a Calder wire portrait hanging in a museum or gallery, you'll see that when it moves, it looks as if it's having a conversation with you. String up your wire creations inside the house and see the subtle shifts they make when the doors and windows are open or when someone walks by. Is your wire portrait watching you?

Stabile

Though Sandy Calder was mostly fascinated by actual movement, he also created wonderfully animated but perfectly stationary sculptures called *stabiles*. These were primarily made of sheet metal or steel and were excellent examples of the physical principles of balance. When you look at them, it seems impossible that they could stay upright. But with a background in engineering, Calder knew what he was doing. His stabiles were abstract shapes, often vaguely resembling animals, or furniture or playground equipment about to come to life.

Using only toothpicks and a few handfuls of marshmallows, you can make an edible version of Calder's magnificent metal sculptures. To assemble, first make a base for the sculpture by sticking four toothpicks into four marshmallows to form a square. Then simply build

Who can play?
Ages 6 and up.

What do we need?
Light- to medium-gauge wire (aluminum, copper, plastic or fabric coated) and heavy-weight clear fishing string; toothpicks and large and mini marshmallows; scraps of wood, wood or wire dowels, light hanging wire, and small objects and simple materials collected from around the house; castoff metal forks and spoons, kitchen and desk utensils, like whisks and round-edged scissors, and a wire coathanger.

Running time?
A couple of hours.

Budget?
$$

When everything goes right, a mobile is a piece of poetry that dances with the joy of life and surprise.

—Alexander Calder
(1898–1976)

vertically from your base using additional toothpicks and marshmallows. See how high you can build your structure, using twenty marshmallows, without it falling over. Challenge the laws of physics by building up from one or two corners only.

Standing at Attention

Old Alexander had many tricks up his sleeve. Aside from mobiles and stabiles, he also dabbled in *standing mobiles,* sculptures that rested on a solid base but had movable, mobile-like elements. You can make any number of homemade versions using scraps of wood, wood or wire dowels, light hanging wire, and objects you create from simple materials or collect from around the house. Look at examples of Calder's standing mobiles, then cobble together your own, using scavenged materials from around the house.

Kitchen Symphony

In the 1950s, Calder found himself sharpening some of his earlier attempts at sound-making sculpture by applying a good dose of both mechanical and sound engineering to his latest creations, called *sound mobiles.* Much like wind chimes, these mobiles made noise when the metal parts of them collided. In some of these, such as *Triple Gong,* Calder included small metal hammers that hit pieces of the sculpture at random. Try a hand at sound sculpture by hanging small metal yard-sale finds and kitchen castoffs—forks, knives, and spoons, safety scissors, whisks, tongs, hole punches, and so on—by varied lengths of fishing wire attached to a coat hanger. Hang near a window in the kitchen and enjoy the symphonic chatter of your piece when the wind blows.

august
paloozas

True Blue

I love every bit of summer, from the frantic joy of the last day of school to the languid last licks of freedom on Labor Day. But perhaps my favorite moment of summer is when blueberry season arrives, and for two weeks or so in August, you can pick 'em and eat 'em until you're, well, blue in the face!

What's the Palooza?

Organize a blueberry blowout, ripe with berry picking and a blueberry bakeoff. Get a gang together and make a date to go blueberry picking. Plan to go early in the day, before the heat softens the berries and burns the back of your neck while you pick. If you have a secret blueberry hill where wild blueberries can be had for the plucking, head for your hill before bears and birds harvest your crop. Otherwise, look for a local farm that features pick-your-own-blueberries—these growers are happy to let you pay to do their work for them! You'd be amazed how easy it is to find a blueberry farm near you. Look for their ads in your local newspaper, on roadside signs, or Google "blueberry picking," followed by the name of your state or county.

The night before your blueberry outing, read or listen to Robert McCloskey's classic children's book *Blueberries for Sal.* It's a timeless and sweet story you'll never outgrow. Hunt down Fats Domino's great version of the 1940 Glenn Miller hit, "Blueberry Hill." Gather some baskets or small buckets with handles for collecting your berries. Most U-Pick blueberry farms provide boxes for gathering berries, but bring a few of your own, just in case.

The best part of picking blueberries is eating them while you pick. You pick a few, you eat a few, you pick a few more. Just when you think you can't eat another, a big plump berry catches your eye, and soon it's on its way to your belly. Blueberries are ripe when they are a dusky blue and almost roll off the stem when you reach to pick them. Choose firm berries that are entirely blue (indigo blue, purple blue, or blue-black); berries with a hint of red or white aren't ripe.

When you get them home, store them in covered containers in the fridge for up to ten days. Don't wash them until you're ready to eat them or cook with them. Watch for berry juice in the container, because that means there's a crushed berry that can speed up the softening of all the berries and introduce mold to the whole bunch. If you know you're going to work with your berries right away, wash them and have at it. If not, you might want to keep a few in the fridge for munching and freeze the rest to use later. Blueberries freeze well; just rinse and completely dry them before popping them in an airtight resealable plastic bag or container.

All-Time Favorite Blueberry Dishes

Blueberry cheesecake
Blueberry cobbler
Blueberry coffee cake
Blueberry ice cream
Blueberry jam
Blueberry muffins
Blueberry pancakes
Blueberry pie
Blueberry sorbet
Blueberry soup
Blueberry syrup

Grow Your Own

There's a reason blueberries are known as the all-American fruit; along with cranberries and Concord grapes, they're the only fruit crop that is native to this country. So grow some! It's easy to grow blueberries in your own yard; all you need is a spot with at least six hours of full sunshine and slightly acidic soil (you can add an acid supplement to your soil to make it just right for blueberries, if necessary). Buy healthy two- to three-year-old plants from a good nursery. If you can, plant two or three about five feet apart. For the first two years after you plant them, you'll need to remove the flowers from your bushes so they can concentrate all their energy on developing strong roots and shoots. In the third year, your bush should begin producing blueberries. Be ready with bucket in hand to harvest your blueberries; you'll be competing with your backyard birds for the tasty treasures. A fully mature highbush blueberry can grow from six to ten feet tall and produce up to six pounds of berries every year. Yum.

the blues, n.: a style of music that originated among African-Americans early in the twentieth century; characterized by a slow tempo, melancholy sound, and the repeated use of "blue notes," which are flat third and seventh notes.

Some people freeze them first spread out on a cookie sheet, so that each blueberry is individually frozen (not frozen together) and then put them in an airtight container for long-term storage.

Blueberry Bakeoff

At any given time in late July or August, there's a blueberry festival going on somewhere in this country, from Maine to Florida and New York to California. Almost every one of them has a blueberry bakeoff, a contest where people enter different homemade goods they've created using the star ingredient, blueberries! These folks love their blueberries, and you'll find everything from classics like blueberry pie or peach-blueberry cobbler to inventive entries like blueberry barbecue sauce or blueberry onion relish.

Get everyone who joined your blueberry-picking expedition to dream up a dish to enter in a blueberry bakeoff! Look for recipes in your family's cookbooks or in cookbooks at the library, or online at sites like www.blueberry.org or www.justberryrecipes.com. Or use existing recipes to give you ideas for creating your own original recipe. Play the Miles Davis classic CD *Almost Blue* while you experiment and test, cook, and bake up a storm. Host a mini blueberry festival in your own home, inviting everyone to come for pancakes and blueberry syrup and to enter their creations in the bakeoff. Invite an impartial judge (or two or three) to pick a winner. Then give him a blue ribbon, of course.

Waterworld

Forget the miles of driving, the bother of parking, and the pain of paying to visit a water park. Set one up on a hot day at home, and your yard will be crawling with kids as happy as waterbugs.

What's the Palooza?

Think of this as a water carnival. And no pool necessary, just water and a few simple items and accessories for your super-soaking games.

Don't Be a Sisyphus

In Greek mythology, Sisyphus is stuck in Hades' underworld, having to continuously roll a block of stone up a steep hill, only to have it tumble back down again when he reaches the top. This contest involves the seemingly futile task of filling a large bucket using holey cans of water. Here's how to play:

Ask your parents to use a hammer and nail to punch several holes into the bottom and the sides of two coffee cans or plastic containers. (Hammer from the outside in to prevent injury and sharp edges poking out.) Place a large tub of water at a starting point. About thirty or so yards downfield, have two empty receiving tubs for each team. For this relay event, each person has to go to the large container of water, dip their can in, and run down the field to their team's tub to deposit the water. Then the player runs back and hands the can to the next person on his team. Give the teams two or three turns going back and forth, the winner being the team that fills its tub the highest. It's not going to be easy, as most of the water will come cascading out of the bottom of the cans as you race to fill your tub.

Who can play?
Ages 6 and up.

What do we need?
Swimsuits, hose and convenient water source, coffee cans or quart-sized plastic containers, hammer and nail, five plastic buckets or wastebaskets, eight small plastic buckets with handles (like painter's buckets), sponges, simple squirt guns, towels, two large T-shirts, lawn chairs, plastic cones or other possible obstacles, four large plastic tubs, two kiddie wading pools, plenty of ice cubes, water balloons, a volleyball or badminton net.

Running time?
A couple of hours.

Budget?
$$$

Liquid Limbo and High Hurdles

An easy-play, easy-drench game that's fun for everybody. With your thumb covering half the opening of a garden hose connected to an outdoor faucet, turn the water on full blast. Invite contestants to go under the water stream, preferably along with some calypso-style music to get the limbs doing the limbo; after everyone's gone through, lower the water by an inch. When a player is hit by the stream of water, he's out.

For hurdles, players must jump over the stream of water instead of shimmying under it. After everyone's gone through, raise the stream an inch. The winner is the person who leaps the highest without getting caught in the stream of water.

Sponge War

Water balloon battles are fun, but there are so many balloons to fill (which takes time), and so much balloon debris scattered on the battlefield when it's over. Use a bunch of big old-fashioned sponges instead. They get nice and sloppy-soppy and are harmless when you bean someone. Scatter buckets of water about your field of play to give everyone easy access for reloading. Set lawn chairs on their side for barricades. Or arrange plastic cones and lawn chairs to create an obstacle course a player has to run through while opponents try to hit him from an assigned distance. Every now and then call a time-out so sponges can be collected from the field and returned to the buckets.

Bucket Brigade

Arrange teams in two lines with the head of the line near a water source, and the end of the line thirty or more yards away, with large tubs at the end of each line. Arrange team members at equal intervals along the line from head to finish. Each person at the head of the line fills a small handled bucket with water and, on Go! passes the bucket to the next person, who passes it to the next, and so on, being careful not to spill the contents on each handoff. The last person in line dumps the contents into the large tub. As one bucket of water is sent down the line, another bucket is filled at the head of the line and sent off. As the pace quickens, water slops all over everyone, making it harder for the full contents of the bucket to make it to the end. The team with the most water in their collection tub when the final whistle blows wins.

Ballooneyball

This is like hot potato over a volleyball net. Fill a big bucket with half-full water balloons. Split into teams and arrange yourselves on either side of the net as if playing a game of volleyball. One team is first to "serve." Server tosses a water balloon up in the air and over the net, where an opposing player has to catch the balloon without breaking or dropping it. That player tosses it back over the net, and players lob it back and forth from side to side until it breaks. When it does, a point is awarded to the other side and a new balloon is introduced. You can even move the team around the court after each serve, the way you do in volleyball.

Towel Toss

You need a minimum of four people (two teams of two) per round of this game. Have two kids grab either end of a towel, put a water balloon in the middle of the towel, and throw it to the other team holding a towel, who has to catch it. Keep tossing and catching until someone drops/breaks the balloon. In every toss, both people take a small step backward. Every dropped balloon is a point for the team who tossed it; first team to 10 wins.

Squirt-Gun Tag

Long before there were Super Soakers and Liquidators, there were simple squirt guns that were just great for a lively game of hide-and-go-water-tag. That's right, it's a combination of hide-and-go-seek and tag. Everyone loads up a small squirt gun with water, then hides. The person who is It (who also has a loaded squirt gun) counts to 20, then goes looking for victims. When he finds someone, it's a quick draw. If the person who is It shoots the hider first, the hider is now It. If the hider hits the person who is It first, he's back to counting to 20 again and then hunting for his next hider. The fun is in hiding well, and strategizing how to be ready with the fastest shot, OK Corral–style.

Make It a Party!

Invites: Blue construction paper cut out in the shape of a wave. "Come to the First Annual August Aquafest!"

Food and Decor: This party is all outdoors (except for brief bathroom runs!) so decor is minimal. Stacks of towels, beach balls, and all your party game gear at the ready. Food is light and cool—watermelon, lemonade, ice pops. When guests get sticky, hose them off!

Activities: Water games, as described. Make the day work like the Olympics: award points for each game, name medal winners at the end. Give prizes for "special" performances—Most Waterlogged, Best Shot in the Sponge War, and so on.

Favors: Bags of water balloons, towels custom-decorated with your water park logo or date and occasion of your party, squirt guns.

Ice-capades

During the winter, mounds of ice as thick as fifty feet can be found at Niagara Falls. Why? The falling water and mist can create ice formations along the banks of the falls. If the winter is cold for long enough, ice can completely stretch across the Niagara River and form an "ice bridge."

For this summer ice-capade, divide into two teams. Have each team get into a wading pool (they can be sitting or standing). Have someone pour at least 25 ice cubes into each pool and say Go! Teams race against a 60-second clock to grab and toss out of the pool as many ice cubes as they can . . . with their feet! The team that has removed the most ice cubes at the end of the game wins.

Sticky Wet

Divide into two teams. Split each team into two, and have each half stand in line next to buckets of water thirty yards apart. Dunk two large identical T-shirts into a bucket of water. On Go! the first person for each team has to take the T-shirt out of the bucket, put it on, run the thirty yards to the other bucket, remove the T-shirt, and drop it in the bucket. The first person at that end takes the T-shirt out of the water, puts it on, and runs to the opposite end. The first team to have every player run down and back to where they started wins. It's really sticky-tricky to put on wet clothing, you'll discover, and everyone will look like drowned rats when it's over.

Slip-i-dee-doo-dah

Make your own backyard water slide with forty feet of thick plastic sheeting (you can get it at Home Depot) and a garden sprinkler. Set the plastic sheeting on a grassy hill that is free of rocks and sharp bumps. Secure the slide at the four corners and at intervals along the edges with small plastic garden stakes. Set a sprinkler on low at the top of the slide to make and keep it good and slickery. Take turns slipping and sliding on your belly or your back, giving yourself plenty of room between sliders. When you're done, remove all the stakes and plastic slide; slippy-slides can be tough on a lawn, so the quicker you get it up, the sooner your grass will be back to green and happy.

Cookin'

Julia Child was an American original and a national treasure. I can't think of a better way to celebrate her legacy than to egg on a new generation to get cookin'.

What's the Palooza?

Long before there were whole networks devoted to cooking shows, chef Julia Child had the television airways pretty much to herself. Her show *The French Chef* first aired in 1963 and was an instant hit, partly because she was so good at making complicated recipes and techniques easy to understand and partly because America was ready to learn about fine food. She had a good-natured way, and with every lesson, she made the home cook feel more confident in his ability to try even the trickiest dishes. Her main advice never changed over her more than forty years as a cookbook author and television personality: If you follow instructions from well-written recipes, you will succeed as a cook. And don't be afraid to make mistakes; they're all a part of learning.

Julia practiced what she preached. She tested her recipes over and over, making sure her instructions were careful and clear so that the cook would have the best chance of succeeding. And she let herself make mistakes right there on her TV show, for all the world to see—with a cheerful "Whoops!" a chicken might get away from her. Or if a potato pancake flopped when she flipped it, she'd patch it back together and keep going. She snacked and tasted as she cooked, and generally made it seem like it was smart, tasty, good fun. Which it really was, argued Julia, if you took the time to learn the fundamentals.

This palooza dips into some of the classic French fare

Julia Child introduced to America, each dish revolving around a friendly, familiar ingredient—eggs. As Julia pointed out, the French don't eat eggs for breakfast, so they've put lots of ingenuity into eggs for other meals. As the French have known for centuries—and Julia let us in on the secret!—if you've got fresh eggs on hand, you can always put something delicious on the table. Here are three egg dishes to master, starting with one of the most basic and working up to one of the most impressive. Two things to know when you're "cookin' with Julia": The directions may sound complicated, but they're really just very precise. So if you follow the instructions carefully, you will discover that what you've made was much easier to make than it sounded at first. The other delightful discovery you will make is that an omelette isn't just an omelette when you cook them like Julia—taking the time to learn to make it her way will yield an incredibly smooth, creamy mouthwatering version of that rubbery thing you might get at a diner. Do it right and it truly will taste like a dream. Now put on your apron and have at it!

The Omelette

The definition of the word *omelette* is scrambled eggs with a shape. How simple is that? The best thing about the omelette is that it's an elegantly delicious dish that's cinchy to make—no more than a couple of minutes, once you get the hang of it. You don't need a fancy pan; any medium-sized sturdy nonstick skillet with sloping sides will do. And have a good potholder handy, as the skillet handle can get hot.

3 eggs
1 tablespoon of water (you can use cream or crème
   fraiche, if preferred)
1½ tablespoons butter
Salt and pepper to taste
Softened butter to taste

Break eggs into a bowl and add the water or cream. Put the butter into the skillet and heat over high heat, tilting the pan in all directions as the butter melts to coat the pan thoroughly. While the butter melts, whip the eggs and cream for 20 to 30 seconds with a fork until yolks and whites are blended. When the butter foam subsides, pour in the eggs. The eggs should sizzle when they hit the pan.

Let the eggs settle for 4 to 5 seconds, then stir the eggs gently with the bottom of the fork while moving the pan back and forth over the heat. When the eggs have formed a soft custard (about 10 seconds), sprinkle with salt and pepper. Now lift the handle to tilt the pan away from you, and fold the top third of the omelette over the middle with a soft spatula. Tip the pan in the opposite direction and fold the near end of the omelette over the middle. Remove the pan from the heat, tip the pan over a warm plate, and nudge the omelette onto the plate with the spatula. Spread with a bit of softened butter and serve with a little green salad, a hunk of crusty French bread, and sparkling water.

Omelettes are infinitely adaptable. You can add chopped fresh herbs, such as parsley, chives, or tarragon, at the same time you sprinkle with salt and pepper (before folding and finishing the omelette). Or you can mix the herbs right into the uncooked egg mixture before adding to the hot pan. You can also add a handful of grated Swiss cheese at this stage, or a couple of tablespoons of good-quality ham or cooked bacon, chopped into half-inch pieces. Once you master the basic omelette, you can have fun playing with fillings and variations.

The Great Crepe Escape

Julia Child believed that crepes should be a must in any cook's bag of basic tricks. Like omelettes, crepes require a minimum of ingredients and time and are easy to adapt, depending on additional ingredients you have on hand. The paper-thin pancakes can be a sweet dessert or a savory meal, depending on the filling you use. It takes five minutes to mix crepe batter, an hour for the batter to rest, and another five minutes or so to make the crepes themselves. If you want to serve them hot out of the pan, have your fillings prepped and ready before you start to cook your crepes, as they finish in a jiffy. Otherwise stack the crepes between pieces of wax paper as they are made and assemble with fillings when you're done with all of them.

You'll need a sturdy small to medium-sized nonstick skillet or a flat crepe pan to make these—your pan needs to be heavy enough to take the moderately high heat and nonstick so the crepe can slip out of the pan easily. Also have a good potholder for handling the skillet and a ladle for spooning batter into the pan.

1 cup all-purpose flour
3 large eggs
$2/3$ cup milk
$2/3$ cup water
$1/4$ teaspoon salt
Butter for preparing pan

In a food processor or blender, mix flour, eggs, milk, water, and salt for five seconds or so, until thoroughly blended. Do not overprocess, or your batter will be too fluffy with air. Pour batter into a mixing bowl, cover with plastic wrap, and refrigerate for at least an hour and up to two hours. When your batter is rested and ready, melt a teaspoon or so of butter in the skillet over moderately high heat, tipping the pan in all directions to thoroughly coat. Flick a couple of droplets of water in the pan; if it sizzles, the pan is ready. Pour a ladleful of batter into the center of the pan. Immediately lift the pan from the heat and tip it around in a circle to distribute the batter over the bottom surface. Set the pan back on the burner, and bubbles will appear in the batter right away. Cook for 30 seconds or so, then shake the pan a little to loosen the crepe. Lift an edge of the crepe to be sure it's browning. Using a spatula, flip the crepe onto its other side and

Julia Child was born on August 15, 1912.

cook for another 15 or 20 seconds. Flip the crepe immediately onto a plate so the just-cooked side is faceup.

For a simple dessert or sweet breakfast crepe, butter the crepe, sprinkle with granulated sugar, and roll into a little cylinder, browned side out. You can use jam instead of sugar as a filling, or drizzle the top with cinnamon sugar or good-quality maple syrup. Or fill with juicy berries or banana slices. Add a bit of shaved chocolate or chocolate syrup to your banana filling, and you've got a banana split crepe!

If you want to be a fancy-pants, arrange your rolled crepes in a buttered baking dish, sprinkle with sugar and a bit of melted butter, and heat them under the broiler for a short while, until the sugar gets a little brown and crusty. Yum.

The Soufflé Shuffle

The soufflé is one of Julia's greatest contributions to the American palate, even though it took her a lot of practice to get just right. She described soufflés as "prima donnas in the kitchen; they have to be baked just so, and served just when, and are always trembling on the verge of collapse. They are the boss of things, not you." She perfected this recipe so that you could be the boss of the soufflé, not the other way around. But remember as you're working on this tricky dish, even a chef as accomplished as Julia Child had to try, try again until she got it worked out. Onward!

First, preheat the oven to 350°F and arrange the rack in the lower third of the oven. For dishes and equipment, you will need:

baking dish big and deep enough to hold the
    soufflé dish
2-quart straight-sided baking dish, about 5 inches
    deep, for your soufflé
sturdy $2^1/2$ quart saucepan
whisk
wooden spoon
large clean and dry mixing bowl
electric mixer, with clean, dry mixing whisks
rubber spatula
good oven mitts

Making a soufflé is a three-stage operation: preparation, mixing your butter sauce, and whipping your egg whites. To start, you need:

$1/2$ tablespoon of softened butter
2 tablespoons of finely grated Swiss cheese

Fill the baking dish with enough water that when you set the soufflé dish inside it, the water comes at least halfway up the sides of the soufflé dish. Remove the soufflé dish from the water and thoroughly dry it. Put the baking dish of water in the oven to warm as the oven preheats. Now rub the entire inside of the soufflé dish with butter, being especially careful that the bottom is thoroughly coated. Drop the cheese in the dish and roll it around to cover the bottom and sides with cheese.

Next you need:

2$\frac{1}{2}$ tablespoons of butter
3 tablespoons of flour
$\frac{3}{4}$ cup of hot milk
$\frac{1}{2}$ teaspoon salt
$\frac{1}{8}$ teaspoon pepper
a pinch of nutmeg

Melt the butter in a heavy saucepan over medium-high heat, then stir in the flour with a wooden spoon, cooking slowly for 2 minutes, stirring all the while so it doesn't brown. Remove the saucepan from the heat and beat in the hot milk with a whisk, stirring vigorously. Boil the mixture over the heat for about 30 seconds. Remove from the heat and whisk in the salt, pepper, and nutmeg.

Then you need:

3 large eggs, yolks and whites
3 large eggs, whites only
a pinch of salt
$\frac{1}{4}$ teaspoon cream of tartar
1 cup coarsely grated Swiss cheese

Break the eggs one by one, dropping the whites into the clean mixing bowl and whisking the yolks into the hot butter/flour/milk mix in your saucepan. Add the three additional egg whites to the mixing bowl, discarding the yolks. Beat the egg whites in the mixing bowl with an electric mixer at a medium speed until they begin to foam. Add the salt and cream of tartar, and beat with mixer at high speed until the egg whites thicken, forming soft peaks when you lift the beater. It could take several minutes of beating for the peaks to form in the egg whites.

Stir $\frac{1}{4}$ of the egg whites into the hot sauce, stir in the cheese, then add the rest of the egg whites, folding the egg whites into the sauce with a rubber spatula, scooping the spatula from below to bring a bit of the sauce up over the egg whites without collapsing them. Continue scooping and folding, working quickly for no more than 30 seconds.

Crêpes Suzette

One of Julia's favorite bits of advice to aspiring cooks was, "No matter what happens in the kitchen, never apologize." You've probably heard of one of the most notable French dishes, crêpes suzette, which was actually the result of just the kind of mishap Julia tried to teach cooks to make the most of. A fourteen-year-old assistant waiter named Henri Carpentier was preparing dessert for the Prince of Wales in 1895. He was supposed to reheat and serve the crepes at the prince's table, along with a sauce made of cordials (sweet liqueurs). But the sauce accidentally caught fire, and flames dashed about the dish. Henri rushed to cover up the error, spooning the remaining sauce onto the crepes and hoping for the best. The prince didn't know the flambé was an accident, loved the drama of the presentation, and asked the young man what the dish was called. Henri stuttered a little and tried to name it after the prince himself, but the prince insisted it be called crêpes suzette after a young woman who was seated at his table.

Scoop the soufflé mixture into the prepared dish; this mixture should fill the dish no more than two-thirds. Set the soufflé dish in the baking dish that has been warming in the oven and bake for about $1^1/_4$ hours. The soufflé has to cook slowly, which is why it sits in the pan of water (also known as a water bath, or bain-marie). The soufflé is done when it has risen to $^1/_2$ inch or so over the top of the dish, the top is brown, and the sides are shrinking slightly from the inside of the dish. Test for doneness before removing from the oven by poking a skewer into a side of the puff; if it comes out almost clean, it's done. To serve, set a warm, lightly buttered serving dish over the soufflé and, using your oven mitts, turn the souffle upside down onto the dish on the counter. You may need to get someone to hold the dish for you while you turn the souffle out. If the baking dish was buttered properly, the souffle will come loose from the dish easily. Serve by plunging a large spoon and fork into the top of the souffle, breaking the top of the puff for each portion. Serve with a simple green salad and a crust of French bread. And try not to beam with pride at your considerable accomplishment. As Julia would say in her happy, warbly voice, *"Bon appétit!"*

Inefficiency Day

I'm in awe of the clever folks who invent things to make our lives easier and more efficient. Can you imagine a world without washing machines or cars or airplanes? Or without the Internet and Google to present us with 1,100,000 pieces of information about "time-saving devices" in exactly .51 seconds? I appreciate convenience, but I'd like to see what a day looks like when we pull the plug on all the gadgets and strategies that speed things up. This whole-family palooza is about s-l-o-w-i-n-g d-o-w-n, seeing the sights and smelling the roses.

Who can play?
All ages.

What do we need?
Time.

Running time?
All day.

Budget?
Free.

What's the Palooza?

From the minute you wake up in the morning until you go to bed at night, spend an entire day looking for ways to do things the old-fashioned way—by hand, on foot, in person. This isn't so you can see what it was like to live in the "olden days"; it's to see what it's like to live *now*, but without the built-in pressure of saving time and filling your day with as many activities and accomplishments as possible. In other words, today you will make your way with little or no assistance from time-saving devices, doing fewer things at a leisurely pace—with the goal of appreciating all of them. Instead of saving time, you're going to spend it.

Start by waking up without an alarm clock. Then make a breakfast of freshly prepared foods—instead of a frozen waffle, mix up a batch of batter and make pancakes on the stove. Oh, and make your batter from scratch—don't cheat and use the instant pancake mix in your cupboard! Avoid using time-saving appliances like the microwave or dishwasher. Do your breakfast dishes by hand in the sink, using the tried-but-true "I wash, you dry" method.

Throughout the day, be mindful of all the shortcuts and conveniences you normally rely on. If you can walk instead of drive somewhere, do it. If you have to drive, take the long, scenic route. And park as far away from your destination as you can and walk the rest of the way. Take the stairs instead of the elevator. At home, sweep instead of vacuum. Hang laundry out to dry on a clothesline if it's a nice day. Put the remote control away—or better yet, skip TV and read or do a palooza! Talk with your friends in person instead of chatting online or on the telephone. Exercise by taking a walk outdoors instead of going to the gym and using the treadmill.

Take the time to use your five senses throughout the day. Use your eyes to take in details that you might normally miss when you're rushing from one activity to the next. Note the color of someone's eyes, the shape of a leaf, the changing

Build a better mousetrap, v. phrase: Invent a product that improves on an existing product or makes something more efficient.

Pancakes!

1$\frac{1}{2}$ cups all-purpose flour
3 tablespoons sugar
1$\frac{1}{2}$ teaspoons baking powder
$\frac{1}{2}$ teaspoon of salt
1$\frac{1}{2}$ cups of milk
3 tablespoons unsalted butter, melted
2 large eggs
$\frac{1}{4}$ teaspoon vanilla essence (optional)

Mix dry ingredients (flour, sugar, baking powder, salt) in a large bowl with a whisk. Mix wet ingredients (milk, butter, eggs, vanilla) in a smaller bowl with a whisk, then add wet ingredients to dry ingredients and whisk gently until completely blended.

Prepare your griddle pan by rubbing a bit of butter across the entire surface. Preheat on the stove over medium heat. When the pan is hot, spoon or ladle $\frac{1}{3}$ cup of batter for each pancake. Cook until bubbles appear on the top of the pancake, then flip with a spatula to cook the other side, careful not to let the pancake fold over onto itself as you turn it. Cook the other side for about half as long as the first side, then remove to a plate. Best served with fresh butter, real maple syrup, or good honey. And fresh fruit on the side (or mixed in the batter) is always nice!

(If you don't have a stovetop griddle pan, go ahead and use an electric griddle. But be aware you're using one of those tricky time-saving devices—and find another way to spend the time you saved using an electric griddle!)

light in the sky. Smell the night air; go to a farmer's market and really smell the fresh fruit, veggies, and herbs. Eat slowly so you can really taste your food. Listen to the sounds of the day (horns, birds, crickets, laughter). And make a point of touching things (a smooth stone, rough tree bark, a dimpled potato, a soft piece of fabric).

At the end of the day, sit down with your family and

Nothing Doing

Elevators? They're great. Washing machines? We'd be miserable without them. Some of the actual gadgets below? Not quite so essential.

The automatic dustpan—no need to bend over to sweep up!

The dishdrawer—a combination dishwasher and storage drawer, so you never have to empty the dishwasher again!

The mini exercise bike—bicycle pedals on a frame that fits between your feet on the floor, so you can "ride a bike at your desk"!

The Earthbox—aka the Garden of the Future; automatically grows veggies, flowers, and herbs with no watering, no weeding, no feeding, no gardening at all!

Robotic lawnmowers and vacuum cleaners—no effort and no human presence necessary!

The bug vacuum—forget fly swatters and newspapers, this cordless device "removes" insects rather than squashing them!

make a list of all the ways you spent your time without saving any. Try to think of the things you didn't do today that you normally would have. Note all of the things you absorbed with your senses. List all of the quick, instant, or speedy time-saving devices, products, or services you noticed in your home or out and about throughout the day—drive-through windows, self check-outs, instant oatmeal, and precooked bacon. Think of ways you can be a better time-spender the next time you celebrate Inefficiency Day.

Literary Monsters

When Mary Wollstonecraft Shelley set out to write a scary story, she wanted to "make the reader dread to look round, to curdle the blood, and quicken the beatings of the heart." Shelley's monster ended up being the gold standard of scary monsters, as frightening on the page as any Alien or Predator you might see at the movies.

What's the Palooza?

Who can play?
Ages 9 to 12.

What do we need?
Writing and drawing supplies.

Running time?
An hour or two to fully imagine a monstrous creation; several hours or even a couple of days, if the spirit moves, to write a story to go with it.

Budget?
$

Create a monster and a story to go with it à la Mary Wollstonecraft Shelley. In the summer of 1816 Mary Wollstonecraft Shelley and Percy Shelley visited Switzerland and became neighbors of the Romantic poet Lord Byron. It was a rainy summer, and the Shelleys, Byron, and John Polidori, Byron's physician, whiled the hours away one very stormy night reading German ghost stories to each other. When Lord Byron suggested they each write a ghost story, Polidori actually came up with the first modern vampire story. Percy Shelley wrote nothing memorable. And at first, Mary couldn't think of an idea for a story at all. But soon it would be nineteen-year-old Mary who dreamed up Victor Frankenstein and his "miserable monster," one of the most unforgettable creations in all of literature.

Shelley's influences at the time were many, from Dante to Darwin; the "wet, ungenial" weather that summer; and literary conversations with her friends about the mysteries of life itself and whether or not scientists might someday bring a corpse back to life. Such musings gave way to an unusual night of fitful "waking" dreams and led Mary to write a story that would seize the imaginations of readers for generations to come.

Monsters from Myth

Scylla and Charybdis: Two female monsters who live on either side of the Strait of Messina, terrorizing passing ships.

Cyclops: A one-eyed shepherd, big as a house, who eats Odysseus's men like popcorn.

Gorgons: Sisters, including Medusa, who have live snakes for hair, scales, and boar tusks. Anyone who looks at a Gorgon turns to stone.

Harpie: A fierce, filthy winged creature with the head of a woman and the sharp-clawed body of a bird.

Minotaur: A terrifying half-bull, half-man monster who was routinely offered Greek maidens and men as sacrifices.

Sirens: Monsters who lived near Scylla and Charybdis; half bird, half women, like the Harpies, they tricked sailors into jumping in the ocean, where they were turned to rocks.

Sphinx: A half-woman, half-lion monster that poses riddles to passersby, killing all who cannot solve them.

Mary Shelley was born on August 30, 1797.

To create your own literary monster, you need inspiration! The best place to start, of course, is to read Shelley's *Frankenstein*. Also think about other monsters you may have read about or seen in movies. Why and how did those monsters come to be? E.T. is lost in our solar system and just wants to go home. The dinosaurs of Jurassic Park are products of genetic engineering. Godzilla? Nuclear tests gone bad. How do you suppose William Steig conjured the beloved Shrek, monstrous to look at but a gentle soul at heart? Does your monster have human characteristics? Does he transform from man to wolf like a werewolf or from man to bat like a vampire? What triggers the monster's transformation? Does your monster resemble something in real life that scares you—bugs, bees, birds, growling animals? Or is your monster unlike anything seen or heard on earth?

Words and Phrases from *Frankenstein*

Breathless horror

Disgust filled my heart

Oppressed by a slow fever

Alarmed

Wreck

Peril

Misfortune

Sudden and desolating change

Fear overcame me

Terrific crash

Heavens were clouded

Ravings of insanity

Miserable wretch

Fiend

Forked and destroying tongues

Gush of sorrow

Dejected

Sorrowful

Feverish joy

Sublime

Transcendent

Insatiable thirst

Compose yourself

Tingling

Days gone by

Tenderest compassion

Demoniacal design

Rapid

Ardor

Chivalrous

Infallible

Causation

Wrinkled his cheeks

Agitation

Horror of that countenance

Palpitation

Mingled

Traverse

Does he have superhero strength, or just a wicked intelligence?

Make up a scenario or story for how and why your monster comes to be. Pretend you are a scientist of some kind, experimenting in a lab, when either by happenstance or on purpose you create an unbelievable monster. Use ominous language to begin your story. Here's how Mary Shelley describes Victor Frankenstein's first sighting of his horrible creation:

It was on a dreary night of November, that I beheld the accomplishment of my toils.

Write a brief paragraph describing your monster's physical attributes. Here's Mary Shelley on Frankenstein's monster:

His limbs were in proportion, and I had selected his features as beautiful. Beautiful—Great God! His yellow skin scarcely covered the work of muscles and arteries beneath; his hair was of a lustrous black, and flowing; his teeth of pearly whiteness; but these luxuriances only formed a more horrid contrast with his watery eyes, that seemed almost of the same colour as the dun-white sockets in which they were set, his shriveled complexion and straight black lips.

Consider the way Shelley used words not just to describe the monster, but to build a sense of dread for the reader. Look for ways to use Mary Shelley–like language in your story.

Next draw or paint a picture of your monster and give the creation a name. Invite a friend or two to invent literary monsters. Read your stories aloud at midnight. Will one of you be the creator of the next great literary monster?

Literary Monsters and their Makers

Grendel: The "grim spirit" from *Beowulf*.

Caliban: The savage slave from William Shakespeare's *Tempest*.

Edward Hyde: "Pure evil," from *Dr. Jekyll and Mr. Hyde*, by Robert Louis Stevenson.

Count Dracula: The vampire from Bram Stoker's *Dracula*

Jabberwock: "The jaws that bite, the claws that snatch," from Lewis Carroll's *Through the Looking Glass*

Phantom of the Opera: The disfigured ghost haunting a Paris opera house, from Gaston Leroux's novel *The Phantom of the Opera*

september
paloozas

Checkmate

I remember the year Bobby Fischer beat Boris Spassky—
it was the first time an American had made it to the World
Championship and it seemed like the whole world was on
pins and needles for the nearly two months it took for the
match to be completed. A good chess match is like that!

What's the Palooza?

Who can play?
Ages 9 and up.

What do we need?
Chessboards and
chess sets. Stop-
watches optional.

Running time?
A few hours.

Budget?
$

Make like the grandmasters and play your chess buddies in a home tournament. Invite a few friends over who share your interest in chess. Everyone needs to have a solid understanding of the game to start with. Set up your tournament as realistically as possible, creating a bracketed lineup of play. Write each person's name on a piece of paper and drop the names in a hat. Pull the names at random to create the pairings for the first round of your tournament. If you have an odd number of guests, the unpaired name gets a "bye" and sits out until the next level of play. You will play out each set of brackets until you end up with a final pairing for the championship.

Set up the appropriate number of boards and chess sets at different tables and plan to begin the first round of games at a particular time and set time limits or *time controls* for each game. Serious tournament games usually have an initial time control of 40 moves in two hours, with an additional time control of 20 moves in an hour to finish the game. A friendly home game might have a

limit of 30 minutes with no restriction on the number of moves. If a game is limited to 30 minutes, each player is allowed 30 minutes to complete the moves necessary to win the game. If a player exceeds the time limit, he "loses the game on time."

Competitive chess is almost always timed using chess clocks. The chess clock measures how much of each player's allowed time is spent. Authentic chess clocks feature two clocks, one for each player, and each with a start/stop button that the players hit when they begin and end a move. For your home tournament, you can set each player up with a stopwatch that he starts when he begins a move and stops when he ends a move. A player's stopwatch must be started just as soon as his opponent stops his watch. (If stopwatches are not available, you can use a watch and mark passed time on a piece of paper after each move.) Real chess clocks are

On September 1, 1972 American Bobby Fischer beat Russian Boris Spassky in the "match of the century" at the World Chess Championship in Reykjavik, Iceland.

Make It a Party!

Invites: Cutouts in the shape of chess pieces. Or on a chessboard pattern.

Food and Decor: Checkerboard tablecloths. Giant posterboard drawings of the six kinds of chess pieces. Poster-sized photos of the chess greats—Bobby Fischer, Gary Kasparov, Anatoly Karpov, Deep Blue! Turn ordinary menu items into a chess-themed feast, and include signs for treats such as Sweet and Sour Scepters (chicken kebabs), small Castle Burgers (à la White Castle), Bishops' Hats (phyllo dough filled with broccoli and cheese), Checkmate Cake (yellow cake with checkerboard frosting) or Chess Pie, a popular southern dessert with a simple filling of eggs, butter, sugar, and lemon juice.

Activities: Your tournament, of course. Make it a sleepover and watch *Searching for Bobby Fischer* after the tournament.

Favors: Mini magnetic travel chess sets. Black and white M&Ms.

There are many chess players who play only to achieve a draw. But a game of chess must be offensive. One must seek the way to victory, otherwise what's the sense of sitting down to a chessboard?

—Bobby Fischer (1943–)

Zugzwang

(zoog-zwang), n.: German for "compulsion to move," describing when a player decides to make a move that creates a larger threat later rather than a lesser threat in the near term.

cool and worth saving up for if you're really into chess.

The idea is not to speed through each game but to pace the rate of play so you can successfully complete a tournament in a reasonable amount of time. The most important thing to remember if you're playing a timed game is to stop your clock when you've completed your move. It's easy to forget, and a sharp opponent will surely not remind you to stop it, as you're squandering your own valuable time. Even a grand master can forget. In the 1987 world championship, Gary Kasparov forgot to stop his clock after his twenty-sixth move against Anatoly Karpov. By the time he noticed his mistake, he had only one minute left and was forced to resign from the game on his thirty-third move. That's a bummer of a way to lose!

Make a big fuss over the championship game of your tournament. By now, everyone who is not playing is watching the final competition, so the heat is on! Have a prize for the winner (something nice like a little travel chess set or something funny like a homemade "Chess Champion" sash or crown). And remember which games were the best, toughest pairings—these are the makings of the chess rivalries of tomorrow!

Rules Refresher

If you need a quick reminder of the rules of the game, or need to bring a newbie up to speed, check out www.uschess.org/beginners/letsplay.php. You can also look at *Chess for Kids* by Michael Basman, an easy-to-follow beginner's book, or *Chess for Juniors* by Robert M. Snyder, for beginners through advanced beginners.

Biopic

I have a photo of my grandmother Ida B. Lithgow that I just love. Every time I look at it, I think I see everything I remember about her—what a great knitter she was, how she loved crosswords and card games, how she would recite half-hour-long epic poems that she'd learned as a child. One good photo can tell a whole life story—that's what this palooza is all about.

What's the Palooza?

The debut of Millennium Park in Chicago featured an extraordinary show by German photographer Uwe Ommer. Ommer traveled around the world taking photographs of families, posing everyone from farmers in Iowa to a chef in Uganda against the same white background. He then wrote a short, vivid description of their lives to accompany the image. Between the photo and the text, he manages to convey his subjects' history, hopes, and unique personality. All the right elements of a good biopic!

A biopic normally refers to a biographical film, usually about some celebrity or important historical figure. Let's palooza that definition of biopic to include a photo that reflects the essence of someone you love and tells their whole story in a single frame. It's Grandparent's Day—how about you choose a certain, special older someone as your subject? It can be Grandma and Grandpa, together or individually. You can choose a great-aunt or -uncle, or even a family friend—any older person whom you know well enough to try to "capture" on film.

The Picture. They say a picture is worth a thousand words. Make yours speak volumes by taking a photograph that shows details that really reveal the essence of

Who can play?
Ages 9 and up.

What do we need?
A camera and film or a trove of family photos; good-quality stock paper, good-quality pen, glue, and a store-bought picture frame (optional).

Running time?
Up to an hour to take or choose photo, an hour or more to interview your subject, an hour to write your text and assemble your biopic.

Budget?
$$

your subject(s)—how they look when they're being most themselves. Your grandma's soft smile and capable hands, rough from seventy years of cooking and gardening. Your great-uncle's penchant for pranks that you can see playing at the corners of his mischievous eyes. You can follow Ommer's method of putting the subject against a white backdrop (use a blank white wall or tack up a white sheet for a background). This frames the subject and forces the viewer to examine the details he might otherwise miss with a busy background. You might also include meaningful props in your photo; if your grandmother loves peonies, photograph her holding a couple of her favorite blooms. If your grandfather is proud of his decoy collection, have one of his decoys posed by his feet. Your mission here is to take the opposite of a school picture, where everyone is posed the same way and smiling blankly. Take several photographs, with variations in poses and expressions. Chat up your subject as you photograph her to draw out those qualities you know and love. You want your photograph to be vibrant, with your subject revealing his true nature.

The Interview. Any good journalist knows that to get the best story, you've got to go straight to the source. Sit your subject down for tea and talking. You may already know quite a bit about him, from your own relationship or family stories. Take what you know, and come up with a bunch of questions that will help you round out the picture: Where were you born? What was your first memory? What was your first job? Did you ever live abroad? What did you want to be when you grew up? What's your favorite smell? Can you name the high point of your life? Get your subject to tell stories about childhood or early adult years. Ask follow-up questions—sometimes the most interesting details come up when you keep probing. You'll only use a tiny fraction of the information you gather, but every detail will enrich your biographic paragraph.

The Paragraph. Tell your subject's story in a paragraph. Choose information from your interview that seems to be most revealing of your subject's personality. The style of the text is all your own: you can be poetic or matter-of-fact, comical or serious. Ommer used carefully chosen bare facts that were tenderly revealing of his subjects. Work unexpected tidbits in with traditional items. Of a photo of Grandma, in an apron and seated in a wicker chair with her dog on her lap, one might write, "This is Maria Abatti—we just call her Nonna. She came to America from Italy when she was six years old. She met Poppi on the subway in New York. He says she was the most beautiful girl he'd ever seen and he pestered her to go out on a date with him for months. When she finally agreed, he cried. Nonna loves her summer herb garden and her little Schnauzer, Otto. Her favorite thing to make is an almond torta. It is a secret recipe she got from her mother, who got it from her mother back in Italy. Poppi loves Nonna's almond torta."

When you've finalized the text that goes with your favorite photo, write it on a small piece of heavy stock paper in your best handwriting. Then glue the photograph and the paragraph onto a larger piece of heavy stock paper of a different color. Consider making good-quality copies at the copy shop—you'll want one to keep for yourself, and probably some to give to others. You can frame

Grandparent's Day is September 12.

The Decisive Moment

Henri Cartier-Bresson was a photographer who was a master at capturing the essence of his subject—his portraits are famous for the beauty and heartbreak and humor they reveal in the slightest gesture. Like the best press photographer, he could tell a person's story in a single shot. But as an artist, he understood the importance of composition; that is, the elements within a photo that help it reach its fullest potential. He had an empathy and affection for his subjects that enabled him to bring out their true characters when he photographed them. He also had spectacular timing; he described this as having an eye for "the decisive moment," the "recognition, in a single fraction of a second, of the significance of an event as well as the precise organization of forms which gives that event its proper expression." Check out some photos from his 1999 show, *Tête a Tête: Portraits by Henri Cartier-Bresson*, at www.washingtonpost.com/wp-srv/style/museums/photogallery/bresson/gal_1-1.htm, or look for the book by the same name, for inspiration for your own biopic photos.

your original biopic with an appropriate sized store-bought frame that you can buy at a craft store, or you can make a frame yourself out of heaviest-weight stock paper.

Multipics

If you're feeling ambitious, try making biopics of every-one in your family for a rich, layered portrait of a family. You can mount them in scrapbook, or better yet, get them copied and bound at a copy shop and give them out as a memento at your next big family gathering. Some copy shops, like Kinko's, can even help you turn your project into an annual calendar, with a biopic featured above the calendar grid for each month of the year. Be creative in your presentation—Ommer's installation at Millennium Park unfolds like an accordion, with photos on both sides of each panel and connected at the sides. You could do the same thing, gluing biopics to each panel of a cut and accordion-folded piece of poster paper. A great tabletop decoration at a big family Thanksgiving, no?

Backyard Biographer

Uwe Ommer took over a thousand photographs and traveled throughout five continents and 145 countries to make his *Family Album of Planet Earth.* You can do what he did, but on a neighborhood scale. Make biopics of your neighbors, your mailman, or your babysitter (anyone who will let you!). It will take time to take the photographs, and even more time to interview your subjects, though you don't need to dig deep for fun information for each paragraph. It can be as simple as a line or two. Of a neighbor, photographed washing his beloved 1967 Mustang: "Mr. Hanks was born in Michigan. He says cars are in his blood. No one is allowed to touch 'the 'Stang' but him." Assemble the biopics in a scrapbook or an album—everyone involved will love seeing themselves in your portrait of the neighborhood.

Gourdgeous

I love gourds. The gnarlier they are, the better I like them. When you hold one in your hand, ask yourself, "If this gourd was a person, what would he be like?"

What's the Palooza?

Every autumn it seems like pumpkins get all the press. Sure, a big, grinning jack-o'-lantern is hard to beat. But how about a shout-out for gourds, those lovable garden goofs just begging for a moment in the spotlight? Get a few gourds, dress them to the nines, and watch them light up like the stars they really are.

Go to a farmer's market or a roadside stand and scoop up a bunch of different sizes, colors, and shapes of gourds. Look for gourds like the bottle gourd, which is big and round on the bottom but with a long neck like a swan. Or the penguin gourd, which is shaped just like, well, a penguin—and is easy to dude up in a little tuxedo, too. The striped pear gourd is cool, already looking decked out in fancy pinstripes. And the warty gourd is hard to pass up, with all the bumps and ridges that will give his face character when you're through with him.

Help yourself to a variety of colors, too, from the many shades of yellow, green, and orange, and patterns like stripes and spots. There's no such thing as the perfect gourd—or should I say *every* gourd is perfect? They're each so different, the fun is in taking what you find and working with its features to make something—someone!—you'd want to get to know.

When you get your gourds home, wash off any garden dirt and dry thoroughly. If you're going to use any paint on them, you may want to use a paint sealer first

---

Who can play?
All ages.

What do we need?
A mix of sizes and varieties of hardshell or ornamental gourds; scraps of fabric, felt, ribbon, lace, tissue paper, pipe cleaners, yarn, glitter, glue or glue gun, markers, paint sealer, paint, and brushes.

Running time?
An hour.

Budget?
$$

Gourds and pumpkins are usually harvested in September.

Name That Gourd

Hardshells
Banana
Basketball
Birdhouse
Bottle
Bushel
Calabash
Canteen
Caveman's club
Dipper
Dolphin
Kettle
Penguin
Snake
Tobacco box

Ornamentals
Apple
Crown of thorns
Egg
Flat
Orange
Pear
Spoon
Warty

Luffas
Dishrag
Hedgehog
Ridged

so the paint doesn't chip off. If you're going to paint a gourd entirely, use a paint sealer and a couple of coats of base coat before beginning your decorative painting.

Decide what kind of characters your gourd will be. A cowboy? A golf pro? A chef? Use scraps of fabric, felt, or tissue paper to create costumes for your gourd guy. Make accessories (eyeglasses or jewelry) with pipe cleaners. Give him hair—glue on a yarn buzz cut or bun. Or use curling ribbon to make a mop of curly ringlets. Use whatever you can to give him charm—scraps of fake fur, Styrofoam peanuts, lengths of lace ribbon, rolls of gauze. Use markers or paint to make up faces—eyebrows, eyes, lips, nose. Work with the natural bumps and ridges of the gourd for his facial features. You can always glue on a pair of googly eyes if that's the kind of character you're working on.

When you've got a cast of characters together, arrange them in a scene. Use one-inch rounds of toilet paper or paper towel rolls to create stands for smaller gourd guys. Use plastic containers of appropriate sizes for larger gourds. Decorate the stands to disguise them if necessary. Imagine bits of dialogue or crazy story lines between the characters. Take photos of your little dramatic tableaux. Turn your pictures into postcards or greeting cards with funny captions.

One-Man Show

Create a single, spectacular gourd character and take photos of him in funny settings. For example, make him a desk out of a shoe box, put a toy phone and papers on the desk, and capture him "at work." Use toys and silly items from your room to create scenes for your gourd. The gourd in the kitchen. The gourd watching the football game on TV. The gourd rushing to catch the bus. Invent a monologue for your gourd character. Is your gourd an Italian waiter? Maybe his little monologue is a funny rant about the clueless customers he serves every night.

What's a Gourd For?

Gourds are a mystery. Related to melons, squash, pumpkins, and cucumbers, they've been cultivated for thousands of years—but you can't eat them! Ancient cultures dried them and used them as musical instruments and utensils, such as spoons, ladles, bowls, and water jugs. Crafty modern folks use gourds to make lamps, birdhouses, sculpture, jewelry, dolls, even Christmas tree ornaments. An all-time favorite use is to make rattles. When a gourd is thoroughly and properly dried, the seeds rattle around inside the dry interior of the gourd.

To make your own rattle, take a small mature gourd with a natural "handle," such as a banana or bottle gourd. You can tell a gourd is mature if the stem has begun to turn brown. Wash and dry the outside of the gourd, handling it gently so it doesn't bruise. Store it in a warm, dry place where the air circulates well. If you're drying more than one, be sure they're not touching each other. When you can hear the seeds rattling inside the gourd—anywhere from a few weeks to a few months after harvest, depending on the size and variety of gourd—you've got yourself a rattle.

Cinderella Fella

Go all out making a costume for a Cinderella gourd. Doll it up with lace and chiffon and ribbons and glitter. Give it a luxurious yellow yarn mop of hair. Then paint a pumpkin white, splash it with a dash of gold spray paint or glitter, put it on four wooden wheels, and Cinderella's got herself a pumpkin coach! Make little mice footmen out of small gourds. And if you're really feeling ambitious, make a Prince Charming, too.

Tilting at Windmills

I have a great big soft spot in my heart for Don Quixote, Miguel de Cervantes's infuriating but lovable hero. As a kid, Quixote inspired me to make a lance out of a broomstick to battle the imaginary enemies in my own backyard. As an adult, he reminds me that we all need to put on a broken-down helmet every once in a while and go out there to right a few wrongs.

Who can play?
Ages 6 and up.

What do we need?
A copy of *Don Quixote*, ordinary household items (pots, pans, colanders, broom, mop, cookie sheet, empty tissue boxes, cardboard, tin foil, string, and so on), notebook, pencil or markers. Video of *Don Quixote* or *Man of La Mancha* optional.

Running time?
An hour, or a lifetime.

Budget?
Free.

What's the Palooza?

After reading too many romantic books about the adventures of chivalrous knights, Alonso Quixada sets off on a quest to right all manner of wrongs and gain fame for his own valorous deeds. "Happen what might to our adventurer, everything he saw or imaged seemed to him to be and to happen after the fashion of what he read of. . . ." When Quixada looks in the mirror, he doesn't see an ordinary man; he sees a brave knight named Don Quixote. And when he looks out on a field of windmills, he sees giants that he must battle. Some people think Quixada's gone mad; I just think he had a great imagination!

Suit Up

Quixada began his transformation from man to hero by donning a makeshift suit of armor. Make like Alonso

Quixada and become the Don Quixote of your dreams. Scour the house for bits and pieces that will become your suit of armor—the more unlikely or zany, the better. Your mom says that's a metal colander? You're quite sure it's your helmet! The broom handle? Your lance! The cotton mop? Your trusty steed. Make a chestpiece of armor out of two big pieces of cardboard covered on one side with tinfoil, attached over your shoulders with string and worn sandwich-board style. Make boots out of tissue boxes, a shield out of a cookie sheet. Your bow? An empty gift-wrap tube. Your arrows? How about straws? Scavenge the house for all the imaginary tools you need to battle the giants and protect the innocent.

Miguel de Cervantes was born on September 29, 1547.

Name Your Hero

Quixada gave himself a bit of a promotion when he renamed himself Don Quixote, which implied a knightly level of nobility. What should you name your homegrown hero? Sir Rantsalot? Don Fernando Spaghettio? Pick a funny name that suggests a little quirk of your character, either in the way it sounds or what it means. What's the name of the noblewoman you used to call Mom? La Duchessa Di-Dolci-e-Latte (the duchess of sweets and milk!).

Sancho and Dapple

While you're at it, now's a good time to enlist a road buddy and partner in crime-fighting. Don Quixote had Sancho Panza, a local handyman who the Don turned into his trusty squire. Sancho, in turn, brought along his beloved donkey, Dapple. Bring a friend in as a sidekick for your adventure. Have him jimmy up a nutty kitchen-closet costume,

tilting at windmills, idiomatic v. phrase: Engaging in conflict with an imaginary opponent. Refers to the fictional character Don Quixote tilting (or jousting) at windmills he imagines to be monstrous foes.

too. Outfit your dog with an elegant scarf and invite him to join your noble quest.

Your Mission

Here's where you choose your adventure. Are you going out to conquer a single enemy—say, that dragon that lives behind the garage? Or is it a journey, like Quixote's, that can take you many places, where you'll face down all kinds of danger or see that justice is done? Maybe you're the defender of animals, and the trees are your imaginary foes. Or maybe your mission is conservation—you police the house to see that lights are off and water isn't being wasted. Along the way, you vanquish wasteful enemies! What provisions and protections must you take with you on your journey? Make a

Good Scoop

Read *Don Quixote* in all its original glory—it's a great book to read as a family, a chapter or two a night. What doesn't make sense to you the first time you read it will seem like a pearl of comical wisdom the next. The translation from the Spanish by Edith Grossman is a good one. Younger readers can check out *Don Quixote and the Windmills,* by Eric Kimmel, and *The Last Knight: An Introduction to Don Quixote,* by Will Eisner. Rent my favorite version of *Don Quixote*—you know, the one where I get to play the Don! This film adaptation is reasonably true to the book, which is another reason I like it. And be sure to see *Man of La Mancha,* a rousing musical telling of the quixotic tale, as well as Terry Gilliams funny documentary, *Lost in La Mancha,* about his failed attempt to make a film of *Don Quixote* in Spain. And check out the video of the ballet *Don Quixote,* danced by the American Ballet theater and starring Mikhail Baryshnikov and Cynthia Harvey. It's fun to look at the various interpretations of the story and the characters in different artistic arenas.

map of your travels. Keep a journal of your exploits—who knows, this could become your epic tale, the *Don Quixote* of your time. Once you set off on your adventure, don't let it end. Finish one "chapter" of your tale today, and then take it up again tomorrow.

quixotic, adj.: Absurdly romantic and chivalrous, idealistic and impractical, caught up in the pursuit of unreachable goals.

Alternate Realities

As with his windmills-to-monsters mirage, Don Quixote sees many extraordinary things, with the help of his wild imagination. To him, a neighbor farm girl is a delicate princess; roadside inns are castles; a herd of sheep is an army; a dishrag is a lady's lacy handkerchief. When he sees a man walking in the rain with a brass basin on his head, Quixote mistakes it for a legendary treasure called the "golden helmet of Mambrino." When you look around your own house, what images of adventure do you see? The television is the dangerous Box of Broken Promises. Your pet guinea pig? The Giant Rodent, whose squeals drive victims to madness. The bathtub full of water for your bath? A raging sea that tests your bravery and cunning. Once you begin seeing ordinary objects for what they *really* are, you'll never get it out of your system.

In Other Words

The language in *Don Quixote* is as rich and colorful as the adventures themselves. Sometimes Cervantes uses over-the-top flowery language or puns for a laugh. He also uses Sancho Panza as a comic tool, having him mangle language by misusing words and quoting endless silly proverbs instead of speaking directly about something. In a single snip of dialogue, Sancho manages to string together "in delay there is apt to be danger," "praying to God and plying the hammer," "one take was better than two I'll give thee's," and "a sparrow in the hand better than a vulture on the wing."

*Good actions enno-
ble us, and we are
the sons of our own
deeds.*

—Miguel de Cervantes
(1547–1616)

This overdose of proverbial wisdom drives Don Quixote to beg, "Sancho, no more proverbs!" Think up your own silly proverbs that sound as if they mean something important. "The fish is fried and the water is boiled." Or "Once is golden, twice is rusty." Keep your proverbs in your notebook.

october
paloozas

Mappa Mundi

Let's give the *Nina,* the *Pinta,* and the *Santa Maria* a rest this Columbus Day. Instead, try to imagine a world without MapQuest and global positioning devices leading us wherever we want to go with our eyes closed. This palooza puts you in Columbus's shoes, with nothing much more than wild rumors and superstition to go on.

What's the Palooza?

Back when Christopher Columbus was a young fellow, a map wasn't a clear accurate geographic representation as we know it. Medieval mapmakers represented their view of the world in fantastic picture maps called *mappa mundi*—Latin for "map of the world." These maps were nearly useless for getting from here to there, but they were a vivid depiction of the beliefs and superstitions of the times. In these maps, the world is, of course, shown to be flat. East, not north, is at the top of the map, and the size and shapes of countries and oceans were distorted to fit the map and to reflect the perceived importance of one place over another. For instance, in the Hereford Mappa Mundi, the only complete wall map of the world to survive the Middle Ages, Jerusalem is shown to be the center of the world. These maps were populated by biblical personalities, like Adam and Eve or Noah and the animals, mythological creatures, Roman emperors, and dragons and other grotesque figures. And a map was meant to show not just place but also time, offering a kind of visual history of the world.

The *mappae mundi* were thrilling to see. The mix of approximate fact and utter fiction they contained must have fueled Columbus's imagination, as a young apprentice at sea and later as an explorer. This could be why he showed up in the Bahamas in 1492, instead of the Far East, where he thought he was going! It wasn't until Columbus and others returned from their famous journeys with real information about distances and geography that maps began to take a more realistic (and useful!) form.

Make a *mappa mundi* of your own town, complete with beasts and mythology and real and imagined people and places. Draw the shape of your town on a large piece of butcher paper (you only need to guess at the shape; that's what your medieval counterparts did!). Think of all the landmarks of your town and the places that are important to your life there—the library, the grocery store, school, your piano teacher's house, the house with the scary barking dog, the three or four streets you consider to be your neighborhood. Mark these with pencil wherever you guess they are within the outline of your town. Here's where reality disappears and fantasy takes over.

Think about all the features of your favorite fantasy stories, from *The Lord of the Rings* to *The Wizard of Oz*. What kinds of treacherous landscapes, magical creatures, secret paths, and mythical terrain might transform your ordinary town? What was once the library may now be the Wizard's Watchtower. Your neigborhood may become a labyrinth or a maze. Begin sketching out your otherworldly world, complete with crumbling fortresses, gates, magical forests, haunted caverns, crystal cathedrals—whatever your imagination imagines. What kinds of creatures inhabit your *mappa mundi* town? Does your cat become a fierce and deadly lion, charged with protecting the Treasure of Tomorrow that's buried in your backyard? Is your sister the mysterious Crone of Cobble Gate?

Now draw in the features and landmarks of your imaginary town. Nothing needs to be drawn to scale—hey, it's a *mappa mundi*!—so your house (your castle or space station or mighty cave dwelling) can be the biggest thing on the map. Or instead of the hundred roads your town is usually made up of, maybe there's

Columbus Day is October 14.

one main traveler's road, and a bunch of mystical little paths leading to . . . your destiny, of course. Drop crazy historical or cultural references into your map—a picture of Albert Einstein or A-Rod or Spongebob. You can cut out pictures from magazines and glue them throughout your map, giving it a kind of two dimensional, collagey quality. Make it beautiful, make it elaborate, make it crowded with architecture and adventure. Pin it to the wall in your bedroom so you can daydream (or night dream) about the fantastic world outside your door. It's easy to get absorbed in creating a *mappa mundi;* you may find that the reinvention of your town goes on indefinitely, as you add new items and features over time.

The Book of Privileges

Christopher Columbus went through years of intricate negotiations with Queen Isabella and King Ferdinand

Oops!

- - - - - - -

Mappae mundi weren't the only maps that didn't paint an accurate picture of what the world looked like. Some early mapmakers mistakenly believed the world to be perfectly symmetrical. To them, the known land mass that people lived on was matched by an uninhabited parallel land mass at the bottom of the world called the Antipodes, which means "opposite feet" in Latin. Others believed in a vision of the world rooted strictly in the Bible; these folks thought that the Garden of Eden was in the Far East, where the sun rises. As a result, these early maps were oriented toward the east, and showed Asia as larger than any other land masses combined.

Even Ptolemy, the great second-century Egyptian astronomer and geographer, had a skewed view of the world. His maps looked believable enough, and he even used grid lines of longitude and latitude that made his geographic calculations seem reasonable. Unfortunately for Christopher Columbus, though, Ptolemy underestimated the size of the world's oceans. Because of this critical miscalculation, Columbus's sailors grew impatient and threatened mutiny when land did not appear as expected. Three days after the threatened mutiny, Columbus and his men made landfall on what is now known as the Bahamas, and the rest, as they say, is history.

of Spain before he ever sailed a mile of his famous voyages in search of China. He made lavish demands, in the event of his success on these voyages, including payment of 10 percent of any wealth that came from his discoveries, and being knighted and named Admiral of the Sea (not too grandiose!) and viceroy of any new lands. The voluminous details of his deal with Isabella and Ferdinand were recorded in a collection of documents known as *The Book of Privileges,* which also included many ordinary instructions, authorizations, and permissions granted by the Catholic Church in Rome.

Make your own *Book of Privileges.* Let it be the official record of all the rules and histories and myths and legends of your *mappa mundi* town. You can use it to tell the stories of all the features and creatures on your map, or as a place to save important documents having to do with your town, such as land deeds, treaties between warring parties, and proclamations of all kinds of things. One of Columbus's requirements, as recorded in *The Book of Privileges,* was to be allowed to carry a royal coat of arms, adapted with symbols such as anchors and waves to reflect his importance to the Spanish monarchy. Create a fancy coat of arms to decorate the cover of your *Book of Privileges.* Use symbols and slogans (in English or Elvish!) that depict features of your *mappa mundi* town.

Fantasy Flicks

Before you create your own New World, you might want to inspire yourself with a screening or two of some of these great fantasy films:

Alice in Wonderland

The Black Cauldron

The Dark Crystal

Dragonheart

Excalibur

Gulliver's Travels

Harry Potter movies

Labyrinth

Legend

Lord of the Rings movies

Willow

The Wizard of Oz

Dictionary Day

If there are three million words in the English language, how come it always feels like the same old, same old? This palooza rains fresh words on you.

Who can play?
The whole family.

What do we need?
A good dictionary, blank notebooks for each person, pens, pencils or markers, magazines and newspapers, scissors, glue.

Running time?
Ten minutes a day.

Budget?
$

What's the Palooza?

Today is a great day to start your word diary, a private place to store the new words you're going to collect this year. Spread the love around—at the breakfast table, give everyone in the family a blank notebook and a turn with the dictionary. At random or with a quick bit of word shopping, choose a word from the dictionary that you do not already know and write it at the top of a page in your diary. Don't pick some big old hard word that's too difficult or unwieldy to incorporate into your vocabulary. Choose a nice, fresh, interesting word, like a ripe apple off a tree, waiting for you to take a bite, savor, and digest.

Take note of the meaning described in the dictionary. Digest it a little and then write your own version of the definition below the word in your diary. Say the word to yourself a couple of times so it feels comfortable in your mouth. Then try to think of a sentence where the word might work. This is just to stretch your brain the littlest bit it needs to make room for this new word.

So I randomly turn to the *Hu–Hy* pages in my dictionary. Do I want *hush puppy* (a little ball of deep-fried cornmeal usually made in the South)? Or do I want *hydrazoic acid* (a colorless poisonous explosive that smells funky)? That all depends! The mad scientist in me wants to know more about that bad acid. But *hush puppy* is a cute one, and sounds like it might taste good, too. I pick *hydrazoic acid*,

When Spelling Counts the Most

Every year around Memorial Day, the country's best young spellers gather in Washington, D.C., to battle to be champ in the Scripps National Spelling Bee. You only have to be younger than sixteen or not passed the eighth grade in school—oh, and a working knowledge of the Greek and Latin roots of words comes in handy, too. These kids are monster spellers; they work and cram and study 365 days a year in hopes of winning the Bee. Do they love the words they spell so well? That's hard to say. They're more like scientists than poets, but you have to believe they can fall head over heels for a really fun, juicy word. Rent the documentary *Spellbound* to get a good look at these superspellers. And go to www.spellingbee.com to get a load of some great words. Here are the winning words of the National Spelling Bee since 1980:

elucubrate	spoliator	chiaroscurist
sarcophagus	fibranne	logorrhea
psoriasis	antipyretic	demarche
Purim	lyceum	succedaneum
luge	kamikaze	prospicience
milieu	antediluvian	pococurante
odontalgia	xanthosis	autochthonous
staphylococci	vivisepulture	
elegiacal	euonym	

because I might be able to use it in a mystery story I'm writing. "The investigator detected the odor of hydrazoic acid in the air at the sight of the explosion."

If you want to, you can illustrate the word for fun. Making it visual is one more way to make the word feel welcome in your head. Be creative in how you illustrate your word—it doesn't have to be a realistic or exact depiction. For instance, how do I illustrate a colorless acid? Maybe just a lab beaker with menacing bubbles coming out of the top. Use crayons or markers to illustrate, or cut images from newspapers or magazines and glue them in your diary next to the word.

During the day, try to use your word at least once, either in conversation or in your writing. Sometimes that may be a challenge—dropping *hydrazoic acid* into the conversation when you're talking to your friends in

October 16 is Dictionary Day.

etymology, n.: The history of a word; the study of the sources and development of a word.

We don't just borrow words; on occasion, English has pursued other languages down alleyways to beat them unconscious and rifle their pockets for new vocabulary.

—Booker T. Washington (1856–1915)

the lunchroom might be a little much. If you can use your word, great. If you can't, just save it in your little word treasure chest until a day when it's the only word that will do. At dinner, report back to each other on how much action your new words saw that day.

Up the Ante

Make your daily word collecting into a family game. Choose your words at the beginning of the day as described above. Make it into a word-busting challenge at the dinner table. Award a point for every time a person was able to use their word during the day. Give a point if the person can spell it correctly. Five points if you can make a little poem using the word and explaining its meaning within the poem. Vote on the day's best illustration. Bonus point if you find your word in the newspaper that day.

It's My Party

There's nothing like the fun, games, and sweet treats at a birthday party. Sometimes, though, a party doesn't look anything like Pin the Tail on the Donkey or a birthday cake glowing with candles. The best party can be super-simple and custom-made just for you.

What's the Palooza?

Help someone celebrate her birthday like she never has before. This may mean it's not a party at all, or there's no cake or maybe even no presents. But there's a lot of thought and careful planning that may just make this the best birthday ever.

When my wife had an important birthday a few years back, I wanted to throw a big party for her, inviting all our friends, who were eager to share in her special day. But my wife didn't want a big party; she was feeling a little shy about her birthday and wanted to celebrate quietly with just our little family. She made me promise not to have a big to-do, and she made me swear I would not have some kind of surprise party. I was stuck! Then I thought about how I could give her the gentle, quiet celebration she wanted, and still allow all our friends to show her how much they care about her. So I planned for a simple, elegant picnic in the park for our little family party. And I asked our friends to write a letter or share a story or a memory or photo of Mary that I could assemble into a kind of Big Hug Book for her. The wonderful tidbits that poured in more than filled a book. And after she enjoyed the peaceful picnic dinner we prepared for her, she opened her present, and the crowd of enthusiastic friends practically burst from the pages of the book. She was amazed and delighted

Who can play?
One and all.

What do we need?
A good sense of the birthday person—and whatever crafty and creative items and ideas you need to make her feel special on her special day.

Running time?
A few hours to plan and pull the pieces together, and however long the celebration itself takes.

Budget?
$–$$$

My birthday is October 19!

and ended up having just the birthday she needed and wanted.

One boy I know loves the Green Bay Packers with all his heart. When he was little, his late October birthday parties were easy. Anything in Packer green and yellow made a good present, and having a crowd of sweaty little dudes over for backyard football and a football-shaped birthday cake was the party. As he got bigger, the piles of little kids disappeared, but his love of the Packers didn't. Fast forward to his fourteenth birthday. What could his family do for this fellow they hadn't done before? Months before the big day, his sisters started writing letters to Packers quarterback Brett Favre, asking if he would sign a football card for their brother. To their delight, a couple of weeks before his birthday, an envelope from Green Bay, Wisconsin, arrived, bearing a football card signed, "Go Pack! Good luck, Brett Favre," for their brother. On the night of his birthday, he downed his favorite meal of chili and crackers, blew out the candles on his cake, and opened the best present a football-loving boy could ever ask for. That's the kind of enthusiasm and thoughtfulness the best birthdays are made of.

Brainstorm a Birthday

What do you know about someone that you could turn into a one-of-a-kind custom-made birthday celebration? Does your sister like to knit? Invite her three best friends over for a knitting slumber party, complete with skeins of fantastic yarn they work with to create something nifty for the birthday girl. Does your dad like James Bond movies? Well, don't just give him another box of golf balls for his birthday. Have everyone in the family chip in on a movie poster of his favorite Bond flick, order some pizza, and have a Bondathon together.

Think about the person's hobbies, favorite sports, favorite music, movies, books, even favorite color. Does your mom love to garden? Don't just buy her a pair of gardening gloves or a potted mum! Use the Internet to search for hard-to-find seeds for her favorite kind of flower. This requires that you know her favorite kind of flower (and if you don't, of course, you should ask!), and takes a creativity and resourcefulness you just can't buy with saved-up allowance. Your sister loves the color purple? Make it an all-purple day, starting with a vase of violets on the table at breakfast to a box of home-made lavender stationery for a present to a blackberry cheesecake for desert at dinner.

Is your dad stressed out at work? Stage what I like to call a "benign kidnapping," to give him a complete birthday break from the everyday grind that will surprise and delight him. Don't tell him what's up. Just have your scheme ready, get him up in the morning, feed him breakfast, then spirit him off to his mystery destination. It can be a baseball game, a cool car show, an outdoor concert, anything at all.

Another way to brainstorm a birthday is to think about what *your* perfect birthday might be. Better yet, don't think about it as a perfect birthday, think of it as a perfect day. What kind of day would make you feel like a Queen for a Day, the belle of the ball, the happiest person on the face of the earth? It's not easy to say, right off the top of your head. But with a little thinking, you could dream up a pretty snazzy day for yourself. Do the same for someone else, and they'll never forget it.

Make Mine a Birthday Story

When you ask people later in life what was their favorite birthday, it's not always a party or a particular present they describe. It usually amounts to more of a story, some combination of people and circumstances that make it stand out in memory. One man I know describes the birthday when his brothers and sisters called a truce on their habitual bickering and organized an all-day, whole-family scavenger hunt. He says he almost forgot it was his birthday, it was so nice to feel like a good, happy family for a day. A writer I know remembers the used typewriter his family pitched in to buy for his thirteenth birthday. He says he was so astonished as he opened his gift, he sat down at the typewriter, inserted a sheet of paper, and hasn't stopped writing since that day. Next time your family sits down to blow out someone's birthday candles, ask everyone to describe their favorite birthday. Collect their birthday stories in your journal.

Teddy

I think it's safe to say they don't make presidents like Teddy Roosevelt anymore. With his (White) house full of noisy, playful children and a great sense of fun and adventure of his own, he brought energy and joyful enthusiasm to the office, the likes of which we haven't seen since. Perhaps we should recruit a candidate from TR's Bull Moose Party and bring the White House to life again!

Who can play?
All ages.

What do we need?
A big raw potato for each person; bandannas in two colors, enough for two teams of people, and a soft football; Wiffle ball and bat; long, thick rope for tug-of-war; binoculars, notebooks, pens, and a camera. Fixin's for a family picnic.

Running time?
A couple of hours.

Budget?
$

What's the Palooza?

Teddy Roosevelt was all about action, adventure, and family fun. So this is a field-day palooza of fun and games played with TR's "bully spirit." Teddy was famous for a kind of hardy, rosy-cheeked, scuffed-knee outdoor play and exploration, perfect for a late-October afternoon. Take a family day to play outside and play hard, because winter is around the corner. Wind up with a simple but yummy fall picnic.

When TR's family was in residence at the White House from 1901 to 1909, his five youngest children, whom he nicknamed the White House Gang, filled the house with games and harmless mischief. And more often than not, the president joined in. The kids once managed to sneak a pony up a back elevator to visit a sick brother. They slid down the White House stairs on serving trays, roller-skated down the marble halls, and kept menageries of snakes, insects, frogs, and rats, all with their dad's hearty approval. In work and in play, TR believed in "the life of strenuous endeavor," and led his family—as well as members of Congress, Supreme Court justices, and visiting ambassadors—on vigorous romps and hikes through Rock Creek Park along the Potomac River in Washington, D.C.

Teddy's Bears

Hunting in Mississippi in 1902, members of President Roosevelt's hunting party tracked a bear into the woods, encircled it, and called the president over to make the kill. Though a serious hunter and a great sportsman, Roosevelt couldn't bring himself to shoot the bear; he thought killing a cornered animal unsportsmanlike, so he put down his gun. Word of the incident soon reached the newspapers; one political cartoonist drew the president with his gun on the ground, his back to the bear, and the words: "Drawing a line in Mississippi." Reading of the incident in the newspaper, a toymaker from Brooklyn, New York (the president's home state), began calling his wife's handmade plush bears "Teddy's Bears." The toy bears were an immediate hit, and TR was good-natured about the whole thing—though he did grouse later that he wished they were called "Theodore's Bears," as he had never liked the nickname Teddy.

President Teddy Roosevelt was born on October 27, 1858.

Fun and Games

Lawn tennis, impromptu wrestling, hiding games, tree climbing, or a session on one of the family's several pairs of stilts might take place on a given afternoon. Simple, silly physical games were favored. See some ideas for your own "bully" afternoon below:

Push the Potato

Everyone looks goofy playing this game. Line the gang up, each with a big baking potato set a couple feet in front. Mark a finish line ten or so yards away, then ready, set, go! Everyone gets down on all fours and pushes the potato to the finish line—with his nose.

Sticky Apple

This is a Roosevelt-era version of tag. And no apples necessary. Just as in tag, someone's It, and everyone else is fair game. When the person who is It tags someone else, the taggee must run to tag someone else, while holding his hand on the spot where he was tagged. Choice tagging spots include feet, ankles, and backs, as holding these spots while running can get a little tricky.

Deerstalker

This is a game that came to be at a time when deer were more likely to be found wandering the woods, not eating the rhododendrons in your backyard. To play, blindfold two players; one's the "deer," the other is the "stalker." Arrange the two players on either end of a picnic table. The object is for the deer to avoid being captured (tagged) by the stalker as they both circle the table. The twist is that hunter and the hunted must play out their drama, as in nature, in complete silence. Observers are sworn to silence, too. Give the stalker a two-minute time limit. If he doesn't catch his prey, he must hunt a new deer. If he does catch his prey, the deer becomes the stalker, and a new deer is invited into the game.

Bandy

This is a game with Native American roots that was played by generations of children until the formal games (and equipment) of field and ice hockey replaced it. Hunt the outdoors for a perfect knobby branch that's thick at one end or has a bend at the bottom—this is the equivalent of your hockey stick. Almost anything that will move can be your puck—a ball of string, an empty plastic water bottle. Mark out a playing field in an open area, with goals on either end. Break into two teams and bandy the puck about in this free-form style of hockey.

Tug-of-War

Just what you'd think. Split into two teams, lined up facing each other, holding firmly to a thick rope. Mark a line that's squarely between the two teams; the first team to be dragged over the line loses. On Go! tug like mad, using your body for leverage as you try to keep your opponents from winning the tug-of-war.

Baseball

Baseball was already becoming this country's favorite game when the Roosevelts were romping in the White House. Play several innings of Wiffle ball or Home-run Derby. Winners get first dibs on picnic booty.

A Walk in the Woods

After your picnic lunch, grab notebook and binoculars and go for a walk in the woods. Teddy Roosevelt was a naturalist at heart; as a boy he'd disappear for days on hiking and camping trips, where he'd birdwatch and observe nature with an intense curiosity. He kept notes of his outdoor adventures, and wrote his own field guides to the birds and animals he spotted near his home and in the wild. Go for a walk together and try to spot something you've never seen before or can't identify—an insect, a bird, a plant, or a tree. Draw what you see, take notes on the details of your subject. When you get home, look in a good field guide (like Peterson's) to try to make an identification. And if you really want to walk the Teddy walk, make a point of visiting one of the many wilderness areas TR so energetically worked to preserve during his presidency; he established 5 national parks, 51 wildlife refuges, and 150 national forests. Go to the

bully for you!
expression:
Splendid! Excellent!
Good job!

National Parks Service's Web site at www.nps.gov for a good overview of the national park system and a complete list of the parks and sights you can visit. And if you're ever in New York, be sure to visit Teddy's pride and joy, the American Museum of Natural History. It may be a museum, but it feels like an adventure.

Teddy Roosevelt, the Human Palooza

What is bully spirit? It's the kind of unbridled, athletic joy with which Teddy Roosevelt lived his life. Buffalo Bill once called him "a cyclone." Mark Twain described Roosevelt as an "express locomotive." A close friend said Roosevelt was really "six years old" in an adult body. Whenever there were games to be played, Roosevelt's children found their father to be their favorite companion and playmate. As a child he battled illness, willing himself well and committed to developing strength by riding horses, playing tennis and football, and swimming. He devoured shelves of books (and went on to raise a household of voracious readers), and explored nature with the seriousness of a scientist. As an adult, TR was just as curious, energetic, and "bully" as ever. He studied science and law, discovered a river in South America, roped cattle at his ranch out west, went on safaris, hiked mountains, became president of the United States, wrote books—and never forgot how to play. Sounds like a palooza to me.

Haunted

Ghost-story aficionados are true connoisseurs—they like their haunted tales rich and sophisticated, no cheap imitations. And they'll hunt down a little-known story like an oenophile on the chase for a rare vintage. Spend a little time with a few of the classics, and you and your gang might just decide to skip trick-or-treating in favor of scaring yourself witless with your nose in a book.

What's the Palooza?

Develop a nose for a great ghost story. Read some of the gold-standard classics—then try to think of your own shivery yarn. And by all means, have a ghost-story party on or near Halloween—not the giggly, shrieky kind but a seriously spine-tingling, sticks-with-you-after-lights-out affair your guests won't soon forget.

How to begin an education in the fine art of the ghost story? Read the best; it's as simple as that. Soon you'll start to know a good one when you read one, and you'll be well on your way to being a "ghosty" yourself. Some great world-famous writers dabbled in the ghost-story genre—Henry James, Rudyard Kipling, and Edith Wharton, to name a few. Washington Irving wrote about more than that Headless Horseman; his "Tale of the German Student" is an authentic bone-chiller. Short-story artist Shirley Jackson is one of America's greatest contributors, as are Edgar Allan Poe and M. R. James. Below is a selection of books and stories to hunt down online or at the library. Read them in the daylight if you have to, but read them.

Who can play?
Ages 9 and up.

What do we need?
A selection of great ghost stories, a notebook and pen, and a flashlight.

Running time?
A couple of hours—or a lifetime, if you get hooked.

Budget?
Almost free.

Halloween is October 31.

Ghost Stories of an Antiquary and *More Ghost Stories of an Antiquary,* by M. R. James

The Norton Book of Ghost Stories, edited by Brad Leithauser

The Oxford Book of English Ghost Stories, edited by Michael Cox and R. A. Gilbert

Classic Ghost Stories, edited by John Grafton

The Mammoth Book of Haunted House Stories, edited by Peter Haining

Some top-notch stories to look for include:

"Turn of the Screw," "The Friends of Friends," and "Sir Edmund Orme," by Henry James

"The Upper Berth," by F. Marion Crawford

"The Yellow Wallpaper," by Charlotte Perkins Gilman

"The Beckoning Fair One," by Oliver Onions

"The House of Sounds," by M. P. Shiel

"The Monkey's Paw," by W. W. Jacobs

"Green Tea" and "Haunted Baronet," by Joseph Sheridan Le Fanu

"Aura," by Carlos Fuentes

"A Visitor from Down Under" and "The Travelling Grave," by L. P. Hartley

"The Phantom Rickshaw" and "The Return of Imray," by Rudyard Kipling

"Miriam," by Truman Capote

"Casting of the Runes" and "Oh, Whistle, and I'll Come to You, My Lad," by M. R. James

What makes for a good ghost story? There's a basic structure to a ghost story that starts with a slow buildup, establishing the atmosphere, offering hints and suggestions of what's to come, and finally delivering the big payoff, the scare itself. The best ghost stories have excellent, vivid details, at least one character the reader can identify with, and perfect pace and timing. Which is one of the reasons why ghost stories are usually short stories rather than novels; the pace of a well-written short story suits the dramatic requirements of a ghost story. It's harder to sustain that pace in a full-length novel.

If you think about it, the reader should never be surprised by the outcome in a ghost story; it is a ghost story he holds in his hands, after all, and a ghost (or two) and a creepy twist is to be expected. Why are we attracted to that shiver we know a good ghost story will give us? Austrian psychoanalyst Sigmund Freud described it as the appeal of the uncanny *(unheimlich)*. On the one hand, we like life to be explainable, ruled by the predictable laws of nature, no surprises. On the other, we're fascinated by unpredictable happenings—eerie coincidences, experiences we can't explain, a vague dread of the unknown. Ghost stories give us that in spades.

Ghostcrafter

So you think you've got what it takes to make your own ghost story? After you've studied up on some of the classics (above), consider some familiar elements of a ghost story you might employ.

The Haunted House. The creaks, the stairways, the dark attic and basement, closets nailed shut. The haunted house takes on a character all its own and is where the narrator or main character has to face her fears. Variations on the haunted house include the abandoned motel and the inherited mansion.

The Ghost Ship. The sea represents the deepest darkness, and a ship on the sea stands for helplessness in the face of that darkness. Picture a ship mysteriously abandoned at sea, without a trace of her crew, or a ship that houses the ghosts of seamen. Variations on the sea yarn include stories involving river spirits, sirens, and haunted wells.

The Dark Forest. Like the sea, the forest represents the unknown and the wildest side of human nature.

True Stories

Strangely, many fans of ghost stories claim they don't believe in ghosts. There's a whole other crowd that totally believes in ghosts and forgoes the fictional ghost tales for the "true stories." These people can't get enough information about real encounters with ghosts, poltergeists, hauntings, and supernatural phenomena. If you're a fan of the "real" stuff, check out these excellent collections:

Real Ghosts, Restless Spirits, and Haunted Places, by Brad Steiger

Ghosts: True Encounters with the World Beyond, by Hans Holzer

I Never Believed in Ghosts Until . . . 100 Real-Life Encounters, edited by USA Weekend

Haunted Houses: Tales from 30 American Homes, by Nancy Roberts

apparition, n.: A ghostly figure, a specter; a sudden or unusual sight.

Leaves rustle, branches snap, tree limbs brush against you. Variations include the modern dark alley in a bad neighborhood, where urban specters replace woodland fears.

The Lost Highway. The highway is somewhere between the dark forest and the dark alley in terms of the fear factor. Variations include the fugitive traveler or narrator trying to escape his past, the never-ending highway, and haunted buildings along a lost highway.

Familiar ghost figures include the Mad Woman, the Long Lost Relative, the Deposed Monarch, and/or Royal Wives. Oh, and children of course, the most haunted of all, and prevalent in the literary spirit world.

november
paloozas

Explorers

Before there were astronauts, space shuttles, and Mars landers, there were Meriwether Lewis and William Clark and their Corps of Discovery, blazing a four-thousand-mile trail across the unexplored western frontier of America. What a pair of American heroes!

Who can play?

Ages 6 and up.

What do we need?

A notebook, pen or pencil, field guides, binoculars, plastic containers with lids, several pieces of shirt cardboard, glue, appliance boxes, duct or packing tape, trail snacks.

Running time?

A couple of hours.

Budget?

$

What's the Palooza?

Grab a buddy and discover the undiscovered right in your own backyard.

When President Thomas Jefferson asked Meriwether Lewis to lead the expedition, Lewis dove into a year of research, studying medicine, botany, astronomy, and zoology in preparation for his trip. As his partner, he enlisted William Clark, who was a well-regarded geographer and mapmaker, as well as an excellent river guide. On May 14, 1804, they set sail from St. Louis on the Missouri River, leading the Corps of Discovery, a group of men engaged to help chart a new course through the western frontier, an area that had just been acquired by the United States. The expedition covered what are now eleven states and more than four thousand miles in about a year and a half, reaching the Washington coast in November 1805. There they built a fort from scratch, and embarked on the return trip in March 1806. When they arrived at St. Louis, Captain Clark instructed his men to "fire off their pieces as a salute to the town," where they were celebrated as national heroes for their adventures in the wilderness.

Prepare

Before you set off on an expedition of discovery, do a little research like Lewis did. Gather field guides to plants and animals and rocks for your region of the country. When Jefferson sent Lewis and Clark to explore the West, he was sure they'd see woolly mammoths and erupting volcanoes. Instead, they discovered something like three hundred previously unknown species of plant and animal, fifty Native American tribes, and the Rocky Mountains. What do you think *you* will see? Pack a notebook and pen, your field guides, binoculars, plastic containers for gathering specimens, and trail snacks in a knapsack. Dress warmly and head out for the wilderness that's as close as the nearest park, botanical garden, or arboretum in your area.

Lewis and Clark's expedition reached the Pacific Ocean on November 7, 1805.

Keep a Log

Assign one of your duo to keep a log of your mission. Captain Lewis was his expedition's leader and official record keeper, but it was Captain Clark who kept the group in line and logged nearly daily journal entries describing in plain words what they saw and did along the way. Clark wasn't the best speller(!), but he had a way of painting a clear picture of what a given day on the expedition was like. From an entry to his log from July 23, 1804:

A fair morning. Set a party to look for timber for Ores, two parties to hunt, At 11 oClock Sent off George Drewyer & Peter Crouset with some tobacco to invite the Otteaus . . . and Paines if they saw them, to come and talk with us at our Camp . . . raised a flag Staff Sund and Dryed our provisions etc. I commence Coppying a Map of the river below to Send to the P. [President] U.S. five Deer Killed to day one man with a tumer on his breast, Prepared our Camp the men put their arms in order Wind hard this afternoon from the N. W.

Observe and Gather

Make detailed notes of the plants, animals, insects, and rocks that you see as you explore. Note exactly where you go; sketch a map of the area you are exploring, marking trees, rocks, buildings, and other features. Record things that happen ("Got mosquito bite in damp area behind the tree" or "Argued with partner about what time to eat snacks") and what you see ("3 blue birds, one with dark marks on head. Squirrel stripping pinecones then throwing them to the ground"). Collect specimens, like leaves, bugs, or feathers, to examine and identify later. When you get home, look closely at your finds and use your field guide to figure out what they are. Affix your specimens to pieces of shirt cardboard with glue and write ID labels below.

Put Yourself in Lewis and Clark's Shoes

The hazards Lewis and Clark and the Corps encountered on their expedition were tremendous. They regularly faced foul weather, illness, dangerous animals, and shortages of food. When they met up with various tribes of Native Americans, they were never sure if the encounter would be friendly or not. Because they could not speak the many languages of the tribes they met, they often used body language and hand signals to communicate. Invent your own silent language to use when danger looms.

Make a Map

When you get home, take your notes and sketches and create a map of the area you explored. This was one of the most important contributions of Lewis and Clark's expedition—the maps Clark made along the way to

New Stuff

Lewis and Clark's expedition recorded hundreds of previously undiscovered species. Think about this: if you're the first to discover something, you get to name it! Here's a selection of well-named plants they found, from A to (almost) Z:

American silverberry

Bessey's locoweed

Chocolate lily

Desert parsley

Edible thistle

Fragile prickly-pear

Great blanketflower

Hair grass

Idaho fescue

Jacob's ladder

Lemon scurfpea

Missouri milkvetch

Nuttall's toothwort

Owl's clover

Peach-leaved willow

Rocky Mountain bee plant

Showy phlox

Tolmie's onion

Umatilla gooseberry

Varileaf phacelia

Wilcox's beardtongue

Yellow bell

share with future explorers. You can make a basic map with markers on paper, or even more fun, make a three-dimensional map using markers on cardboard, Sculpey, and other doodads to represent trees and rocks. You can look at maps from Lewis and Clark's expedition at www.nationalgeographic.com/lewisandclark/.

Great Pairs

Lewis and Clark are one of history's greatest partnerships, their names forever linked, one rarely mentioned without the other. Below are twenty more notable duos—can you think of more?

Abbott and Costello
Fred Astaire and Ginger Rogers
Batman and Robin
Bert and Ernie
Charlie Brown and Snoopy
Frodo Baggins and Sam Gamgee
Gilbert and Sullivan
Gumby and Pokey
Sherlock Holmes and Dr. Watson
Chet Huntley and David Brinkley
Steve Jobs and Steve Wosniak
Lone Ranger and Tonto
Mickey Mantle and Roger Maris
Rudolf Nureyev and Margot Fonteyn
Romeo and Juliet
Romulus and Remus
Sears and Roebuck
Tom Sawyer and Huck Finn
Tweedledum and Tweedledee
Woodward and Bernstein

Werner and Howard who were sent for salt on the 23rd have not yet returned, we are apprehensive that they have missed their way; neither of them are very good woodsmen.

—From the journal of Captain Meriwether Lewis, January 26, 1806

Monet

Claude Monet once said, "I perhaps owe having become a painter to flowers." I know just what he meant by that. How often it is that some simple bit of beauty catches the eye, flickers in the imagination, and inspires all manner of creativity!

What's the Palooza?

It's not enough to stop and smell the roses—you have to look at them thoughtfully, in the light of day, to really take an impression of their beauty. It was all the varying shades of the light of day on his lovely gardens in Giverny, France, that captivated painter Claude Monet. Monet was one of the founders of the Impressionist movement in French painting, a period of about thirty years in the late nineteenth century. Monet and like-minded artists broke from tradition and tried to depict their own visual sensations, or "impressions," of scenes and objects observed in *en plein air* (in the open air). Every painting an Impressionist made challenged their critics—and there were plenty back then—to acknowledge that it's not the thing I am painting, it's *my impression* of the thing. These artists became less and less concerned with creating a realistic representation of what they saw, and more concerned with showing the effects of light and movement on their impression of the objects they observed. And by breaking through the boundaries of strict realism that had informed art until then, these important painters, of which Monet was considered the most definitive, gave birth to modern art. Not a bad contribution!

Painting Expedition

First, do a little armchair-gallery tour of some Impressionist art to familiarize yourself with the way they created original colors to capture their impressions, loosened up their brushstrokes to break free of traditional forms, and used quick brushwork to suggest the movement in nature. Check out *Eyewitness: Impressionism,* by Jude Welton, which is a great, short introduction to the Impressionists. Also look for *The Great Book of French Impressionism,* by Diane Kelder, which is loaded with more than 240 color images, and go to the National Gallery of Art's wonderful virtual gallery of Impressionism from museums around the world (www.nga.gov/collection/gallery/gg86/gg86-main2.html).

Although Monet worked with oil-based paints, we'll work with acrylics or watercolors, for the sake of convenience. Now tuck an easel, paper, and your paint set under your arm and head outside to explore what you see—and how you feel about what you see—in the Impressionist style. Find a spot in your backyard or the park where you can set up in front of a scene or object that interests you. It can be a single tree or a grove of

Claude Monet was born on November 14, 1840.

Make It a Party!

Invites: Postcards of famous Impressionist paintings, such as one of Monet's water lilies, van Gogh's sunflowers, or Degas's dancers. "Join our Impressionist painting expedition in the country."

Food and Decor: This party takes place outdoors, in the backyard or at a park or other natural location. A Provençal-style tablecloth for a picnic blanket and accoutrements for a picnic are all that's required. Oh, and smocks and berets, to get in the mood. Serve fruit, baguettes, and good cheese. Fruity sparkling water would be nice.

Activity: A painting expedition! Take easels, lots of paper, paints, brushes, water, rinse cups, and rags. Once you reach your destination, arrange the easels within sight of one another, each guest choosing a subject or vista to explore.

Favors: Little portable paint sets and pads. Impressionist postcards. A paperback copy of *Linnea in Monet's Garden,* by Cristina Bjork and Lena Anderson.

them, a bed of flowers or a single bloom, a body of water—or even a puddle! You can also focus on an object that is within a natural scene, like a chair or bench, a ladder against a barn wall, or a stone-paved walkway. Choose something that holds your interest and rewards your attention as you try to depict your impression of it.

Think about the quality of the light of the day and how it affects what you see. Is it the thick, sunless light of a winter day before it snows? Is it the bright, hot light of high summer? The muted light of an overcast morning? The warm light of a late fall afternoon? How do you think the light affects the colors and even the shapes of what you see? On a bright, clear day, colors are sharp and shapes are distinct. Other kinds of light can dilute or transform what may be "true" on another kind of day.

Good things to think about as you paint like an Impressionist:

Don't labor over every detail to make it "real." Instead, move kind of quickly, trying to literally cap-

The Accidental Discovery of Color Theory by a Poet

In color as in music, there are countless tones, harmony, dissonance, and chords. Legend has it that the great eighteenth-century German poet (Johann Wolfgang von) Goethe discovered the underlying relationships—the music—between colors accidentally. One morning he was shopping for bolts of cloth and noticed that the red fabric bordered with green was more expensive than plain red. Slyly, the cloth vendor explained to him that he could charge more for those red fabrics with a green edge, because the contrast gave the illusion that the red was more vibrant. The dyer himself had invented the trick by accident, after spilling green dye on red cloth and noticing the positive effects of its contrast. Fascinated, Goethe set out to study the relationships between colors and performed a remarkable series of experiments proving that color was not a fixed property, but was affected by our perceptions of it. Goethe's *Theory of Color,* published in 1810, became an influential text for scientists. It also planted the seeds of revolution among the artists who would become the Impressionists. Decades later, Monet took what Goethe proved on paper to the canvas, experimenting with the relationships between colors to illustrate his own perceptions. Thanks to the poet and the painter, color would never be the same.

ture what you see and feel as you see and feel it. Work your brush loosely, perhaps in thick strokes, as Vincent van Gogh did, or more minutely, as Alfred Sisley did. Camille Pissarro advised, "Do not define too closely the outline of things; it is the brush-stroke of the right value and color which should produce the drawing."

Mix colors as you work. Before the Impressionists, painters mixed their colors in advance of working on a painting and used just the colors they had prepared. Monet painted in a limitless multitude of colors he saw in nature. Grass wasn't just green, and violets weren't just purple; he saw a dozen colors when he looked at the sky and mixed them liberally right on the canvas as he painted.

Revisit your subject. One of the most interesting parts of exploring the effect of light on something is to come back to observe it at different times of day or in different seasons or in light of a different quality. If you did a summertime painting of the old wooden swing that hangs from an oak in your grandma's backyard, come back and paint it again in the dead of winter to see how your impression of your subject has changed.

How Impressionism Got Its Name

Even though he was sort of the Grand Marshal of the Impressionist parade, Claude Monet did not give the movement its name. He did have an inadvertent hand in it, though. Reacting to Monet's *Impression: Sunrise,* an angry critic raged, "Impression! Wallpaper in its embryonic state is more finished!" Soon critics began unkindly referring to this group of experimental painters as "Impressionists," and the name stuck.

Signature Subjects

Most of the Impressionist painters had favorite subjects they painted over and over again. Monet had his water lilies and haystacks. Edgar Degas loved to depict dancers. Alfred Sisley was fascinated by rivers, and Paul Cézanne had a particular fondness for the mountains near his home. Vincent van Gogh favored irises and sunflowers.

Pick a subject that interests you. Maybe it's a giant tree stump in your backyard, or your bike leaning against the side of the garage, or the view of the rooftops from the kitchen window in your apartment. Try painting it at different times of day, with a different dominant color. Then return when you're in a different mood. You could make an infinite number of images from one subject!

I, Curator

Is the weather too funky to go outside and paint? Then stay inside and pretend you've been asked to curate an Impressionist exhibit at a famous museum. Pick a theme for your exhibit—paintings that have something in common (flowers or buildings, or landscapes from a certain season of the year). You can also do a mini-re-creation of the first exhibit of Impressionist art in 1874, the show that started it all. Go to www.artchive.com/74nadar.htm for a nice sampling of art from that collection. Or choose from the world's best collections of Impressionist art for your exhibit. Check out these Web sites for images of the Impressionists' greatest paintings:

www.impressionism.org
www.art.koti.com.pl/index_en.html
www.artcyclopedia.com/history/impressionism.html

Now make your own exhibit. Print out the images you've chosen to be included, then figure out how you want to group them. Commandeer a hallway and/or a big wall to arrange your exhibit. Create brief identification cards for each piece, noting the full name of the painter, the name of the painting, the year it was painted, and the collection to which the painting belongs. Finally, stage an opening where your family tours the exhibit. Collect their feedback and ideas to save for your next show—you know, on comic-book art or primitive sculpture!

Alphabet Soup

It's amazing to think that someone could grow up to be a font designer—a font artist!—dreaming up new ways to present the alphabet. Who says no one writes letters anymore!

What's the Palooza?

Fool around with fonts, dabble in the ancient art of illumination, and reinvent the monogram. People have been playing around with letters since the advent of writing, when the earliest letters were actually pictographs. That was when letters were evolving, when the world's alphabets were taking shape on cave walls and rock tablets. Nothing's written in stone anymore, and today the style of a letter can change at the click of a mouse. If the letters of the alphabet are the tools we use to build words and communicate, what does a font do?

Font Factory

A font is a complete set of letters, numbers, and symbols of a specific size and design. If letters are the tools, then a font is the *style* of the tools. Think about how a font affects how you perceive what you're reading. A straightforward, businesslike font suggests that what you're reading is serious. An elaborate font, with lots of swoops and curls, sends a fancy signal. A round-edged font suggests youth and fun—look at the font for the word *palooza* on the cover of this book, for example. This is a font we created just for this word, just for this book, in order to send a message that this is a fun word and this is a fun book.

Who can play?
Ages 9 and up.

What do we need?
Paper, markers or crayons, magazines and newspapers, access to a computer and printer.

Running time?
An hour or so.

Budget?
$

serif, n.: A fine line at the end of the main strokes of a letter, a defining feature of typography.

sans serif, n.: A typeface in which there are no serifs.

Take a piece of paper and markers and write the word *palooza* in a few different styles and sizes. Or type it into your computer, then highlight it and change the font, using the fonts available in your word-processing program. Try *palooza* in the Apple Chancery font:

$$Palooza$$

Pleasant, but not quite the same sense of fun, is it? How about in Herculaneum?

$$PALOOZA$$

It's downright mythological!

To get a good sense of the power of a font in sending messages beyond the meaning of a word itself, spend a few minutes flipping through a newspaper or magazine. Look at the fonts used in the text for regular articles. Now look at the fonts used in advertisements. How are they different? Are the advertisers using fonts to reinforce their selling message? If they're not, they should be! How are the fonts used in headlines different from regular text fonts? Does the headline font help get your attention?

Using the variety of fonts on your computer, try out a single word (not *palooza*) that has a very distinct meaning—*architecture* or *mathematics* or *poetry.* See the ways a font can "match" or "clash" with the meaning of a word.

Illuminate Me

Back before Johannes Gutenberg invented the printing press in 1440, every book was handwritten, usually by monks in monasteries who had a lot of patience and a steady hand. Think how tedious to just copy the hundreds of pages of a book someone else had already written! The monks kept it interesting by making beautiful art out of single letters, often the first letter or page of a chapter or paragraph. They decorated the letters with ornamental designs, spectacular miniature illustrations, or brilliant colors or gold leaf. Go to www.gallery.euro web.hu/html/zgothic/miniatur/ to look at a wide variety of illuminated manuscripts from 1150 to 1550. Look at all the rich detail that went into each hand-painted page. Examine the decorative and the illustrative elements the artists used.

Now illuminate a word or sentence of your own. Fill an entire page with your work, oversizing an initial letter and decorating or illustrating inside the letter and all around the page. For example, to illuminate the word *apple,* you might fill your most artful *A* with a whole apple orchard or just-baked apple pies. You can play off the meaning of the word this way, or just decorate with flourishes and color.

Poetic License

Some letters of the alphabet seem to convey something more than sound. Poet Arthur Rimbaud wrote a sonnet called "Voyelles," which means "vowels" in French. In his provocative poem, Rimbaud assigned colors to vowels, with black for *"A,"* white for *"E,"* red for *"I,"* blue for *"O,"* and green for *"U."* Other poets have experimented with words and letters as sense triggers, a process that is called synaesthesia. Charles Baudelaire wrote in his poem, "Correspondences,"

Like long echoes that mingle from far away,
In profound and shadowy unity,
As vast as night and like clarity,
Perfumes, colors, and sounds respond to one another.

Write or type oversize letters of the alphabet and think about what color might be associated with each letter (here's where a fat box of fresh Crayolas would be nifty to have). Or think about what the letter *Q* might smell like. Write a short poem incorporating some letter/color or letter/sense associations.

Monogram

Sixteenth-century German artist Albrecht Dürer created perhaps the most famous monogram of his own initials, *A* and *D*. His mark, a *D* straddled by a larger *A*, became almost a logo, an instant identifier of the woodcuts, engraved prints, and paintings of this great Renaissance master. Go to www.ibiblio.org/wm/paint/auth/durer/st-michel/ and look at Dürer's famous woodcut of Saint Michael. Click on the image to enlarge it, then look at the bottom center of the picture for the notorious monogram.

Sit down with a piece of paper and markers and invent your own distinctive mark. Play with style—are the letters capitalized or lower-case? Are they the same size or different? Are they linked or separate? Noodle around with your initials and create a monogram that, like Dürer's, becomes the logo for the one-and-only you.

How to Become a Font Inventor

Before there were computers, typeface designers created types (or fonts) that print shops used when "setting type" to print written material. There weren't millions of typefaces because it was a lot of work to create the blocks of type and change them by hand in the print process. For years, the masters of type were Claude Garamond (sixteenth century) and Giambattista Bodoni (eighteenth century). Now it seems as if everyone is a font designer, and typeface has turned into an art form. Today's typefaces have evocative names like Mrs. Eaves, Cézanne, and Powerhouse, which pretty much suggest visually what the names imply. Go to www.typography.com to sample some of designers Hoeffler & Frere-Jones's classic work. Or go to www.houseind.com to get a load of some "supremely stylish typography." Sometimes the best thing about a font is what it's called. If your signature was a font, what would it be called?

Little Women

What is it about the story of Jo March and her sisters that continues to captivate girls today? Could it be that the virtues of compassion, hard work, family loyalty, and spirited independence still ring true in their twenty-first-century hearts?

What's the Palooza?

Gather a few friends—and fellow *Little Women* lovers—and transport yourself to the days of the March sisters. Imagine a time when entertainment wasn't electronic, when meals and gifts were homemade, when a perfect afternoon was spent reading and talking, sewing and daydreaming.

Get in the mood by rummaging through dress-up clothes to create a nineteenth-century outfit. A simple blouse, a long skirt, and a ribbon in your hair is all you need.

Glove Love

Do you remember the scene in the book where Meg and Jo are at a party, and Jo dirties her gloves, so Meg lends her one of hers? Pretty gloves were one sign of a well-brought-up young woman. Arrange everyone around a table and give each a pair of plain cotton gloves. Set out dishes of buttons, ribbons, rickrack, appliqués, lace, or any kind of decorative tidbits with which to fancy up plain gloves. Affix items with needle and thread or glue gun.

Castles in the Air

One afternoon early in the book, the March sisters and their friend Laurie are enjoying the autumn sunshine and daydreaming about "castles in the air"—the places they want to live and what kinds of lives they want to have one day. Said Laurie,

After I'd seen as much of the world as I want to, I'd like to settle in Germany and have just as much music as I choose. I'm to be a famous musician myself, and all creation is to rush to hear me. And I'm never to be bothered about money or business, but just enjoy myself and live for what I like. That's my favorite castle.

And Jo described hers:

I'd have a stable full of Arabian steeds, rooms piled high with books, and I'd write out of a magic inkstand, so that my works should be as famous as Laurie's music. I want to do something splendid before I go into my castle, something heroic or wonderful that won't be forgotten after I'm dead.

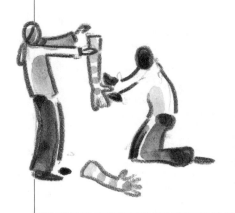

Always a Writer

Louisa started writing at age eight, when she wrote this poem about a bird she found in her yard.

"To the First Robin"

*Welcome, welcome little stranger,
Fear no harm, and fear no danger;
We are glad to see you here,
For you sing "Sweet Spring is near."
Now the white snow melts away;
Now the flowers blossom gay:
Come, dear bird, and build your nest,
For we love our robin best.*

Go around in a circle and have each person describe their "castle in the air"—the best kind of future they could dream for themselves. Like the Marches and their friend, promise to meet again in ten years and see how much closer to your dreams you've come.

Rigamarole

A common group game at the time of our story was Rigamarole, which was certainly the kind of game Jo would love. Sit your group in a circle and choose one person to start a story. The next person adds to the story and on and on around the circle, as many times as it takes for the story to come to a conclusion. The trick? You have to make sure the end of the story is told by the person who began the story in the first place.

Act Out

In the second chapter of *Little Women,* Jo writes a play that she and her sisters perform for their guests at Christmas. Choose a favorite scene or two from *Little Women* to act out. Assign roles, review the scene and dialogue, and put on an impromptu performance. Perhaps it's dramatic, like the scene where Jo sells her beautiful hair to pay for Marmee's trip. Or the sad scene where Beth is so sick. Or even the "castles in the air" scene, where each of the characters reveals so much of themselves. Everyone has a favorite March sister character—choose yours and read a single swatch of good dialogue.

Post Office

The Marches had a little post office in their home, with slots assigned to each member of the family where notes and messages—real and prankish—were squirreled away for each other. Make a postbox out of a large shoe box. Use pieces of shirt cardboard to make mail slots. Decorate labels for each person's slot.

Movie and Snacks

Settle in for a screening of *Little Women,* either George Cukor's 1933 original, starring Katharine Hepburn as Jo, or the 1994 version, which featured Wynona Rider as Jo and Susan Sarandon as Marmee. Serve popcorn, candied apples, doughnuts, and cider. Better yet, have a sleepover and make the candied apples and doughnuts from scratch for fun.

december paloozas

Wegmania

Everybody knows artist/photographer William Wegman's famous Weimaraners—sleek, gorgeous dogs feigning utter disinterest as they pose in diamonds, elephant tusks, platinum blond wigs, top hats, and astronaut gear. This palooza asks you to turn a Wegmanesque eye on your own pet, looking for all the heart and humor the photographer discovered in his dogs.

Who can play?
Ages 6 and up.

What do we need?
A camera, props and costume accessories, an agreeable pet (or a stuffed animal, doll, or a willing younger sibling).

Running time?
A couple of hours, or as long as your subject interests you!

Budget?
$$

What's the Palooza?

You don't have to be a dog lover to appreciate the wry, witty way Wegman poses and photographs his dogs. His own offbeat sense of humor is reflected in every picture, but so is the personality of each of the dogs. Check out some of Wegman's books at the library, and visit www.wegmanworld.com to study his work. Then stage photographs of your own pet in the Wegman manner.

Personality Portraits

Start by taking simple unstaged photographs that explore the expressions on your pet's face or the quirky ways he sits or carries himself. How would you describe your dog's personality? Is he bright and cheerful, sweet, nervous, or a little loony? Take time to look for ways to capture these aspects of his personality in photographs.

Now think of ways to use props or costumes to play up your pet's nature. Does your dog act like a toughie, barking and puffing out his chest when a delivery man comes to the door? Dress him in a muscle-man T-shirt and pose him next to a pair of barbells. Is your lovely cat fussy and aloof? Put her in a high lace collar and brooch, sipping milk from a porcelain teacup, and she'll show herself for the high-society lady she really is. Create different portraits of your pets that capture different traits.

The idea is not to make fun of your pet. As funny as Wegman's photographs can be, he's very careful not to mock his dogs when he stages scenes or poses them. He has tremendous respect for his subjects and knows that they're working as hard as he is to make their art. When he sets up for a funny photo, he is imagining the humorous impact of the photograph, and his dogs are simply playing a part in its creation.

William Wegman's birthday is December 2.

Surreal Compositions

Sometimes Wegman photographs his dogs without costumes, instead posing them for surreal or bizarre effect, alone or in combination, using plain backgrounds and simple props like a stool or a box. There's a famous photo called *Dusted* (look at it on www.wegmanworld.com/art-manray) that features his first dog, Man Ray, in full-body profile against a dark background, with a shower of dust pouring down on his head. Don't try this at home (!), but do appreciate the mysterious effect of this photo. Also check out *Paw*, which features one dog lying flat on the floor, head down and face into the camera, while a dog outside the frame reaches in and rests his paw on the lying dog's forehead. What does the dog's facial expression say to you?

Story Time

Sometimes Wegman's photos illustrate something specific, such as the ones in his books *ABC* or *1–2–3*, where he poses the dogs in the

shapes of letters or numbers. Sometimes he stages a single scene or shot (a wedding portrait, with one dog dressed in white gown, the other in a tux) or creates a series of pictures to tell a story (as in *Wegman's Mother Goose* or *Little Red Riding Hood.*) Think of stories you'd like to tell with staged photos of your pet. It can be a familiar story, like a fairy tale, or a story of your own.

A young friend of mine made up a funny story where his dog was a superhero who "saves" all of his other pets (cats, guinea pig, lizard) from the sinister pet sitter who comes when the family is on vacation. The boy made a crazy cape and mask for his dog and took pictures of him with all of the other animals in little scenes around the house. One of Wegman's original stories is *Chip Wants a Dog,* a book that features photos of a dog named Chip (who doesn't know he's a dog), daydreaming about how great it would be to have a dog. Chip's parents (also dogs) won't allow him to have a dog (his mom is a "cat person" and his dad thinks dogs are "too much responsibility"). Don't forget that clever text accompanying funny photos makes for an irresistible story.

Signature Subjects

Photographers usually have a subject they are known for—people or plants or sunsets or covered bridges. Annie Liebowitz is known for her elegant portraits of celebrities; Ansel Adams for his brooding, majestic landscapes; Alfred Stieglitz for his skycrapers and other architectural icons. It took William Wegman several years before he discovered his signature subject. When he started out in the 1960s, Wegman was a conceptual artist working with video, performance, and installation art. After a while, he began to see his subjects strictly in photographic terms, and then, as Wegman describes it, "In 1970, I got a dog and he turned out to be very interested in video and photography as well."

In 1979, the Polaroid Corporation invited Wegman to try out a new camera, the Polaroid 20x24, a large, complicated camera designed to take life-size portraits. He tested this technology with photographs of Man Ray, and the combination of artist, medium, and subject magically clicked. Wegman photographed Man Ray until the dog's death in 1982 and didn't resume a canine collaboration until 1986, when he became involved with another Weimaraner he named Fay Ray, who also became a star. Thanks to his pooches and his Polaroid, Wegman's work hangs in museums and collectors' galleries and is cherished by adults and children everywhere.

All of this requires, of course, that your pet be willing and calm enough to let you do this staging and costuming. This may take some time and practice, but the more calmly and matter-of-factly *you* behave as you work, the more likely your pet is to become an agreeable subject. Most pets crave your loving attention, and they will eventually see this as the treat they earn when they work with you. Real treats (used in moderation) can also be very convincing!

Finally, if your pet is just not suited to this sort of interaction—or you don't have a pet at all!—look for another model you can use to create similar scenes and studies. You can costume and make scenes for a favorite stuffed animal or doll. Or even better, enlist an enthusiastic younger brother or sister to pose in your Wegmanesque pieces.

I remember spending some time for the first time with Man Ray, my first dog. I didn't talk that day. I just listened to what he was listening to, the whole aura of smells and sounds and sights and things that he was picking up on during that day. Most people who have dogs see them as their dogs: "Come on, boy," or "Fetch" or pat, pat. But they're really teeming with their own thoughts.

—William Wegman (1943–)

Pinup Pets

Stage photographs of your pet to illustrate the months of the year—with a knit cap and skis for January, a flag and sparklers for July, a ghostly sheet over his head for October. Use a computer program to turn the photos into greeting cards or to create a twelve-month calendar. (You can also take it to Kinko's to assemble and produce copies.) Give it to family members as a holiday gift. Make it an annual tradition everyone looks forward to.

Fly, Baby!

Ah, flight. It celebrates itself every time a hawk glides across the sky or a jumbo jet makes a smooth landing. It's one of the all-time great human accomplishments, but what a genie those Wright brothers let out of the bottle—it didn't satisfy our craving to fly, it merely whetted our appetite!

The Wright brothers' first flight took place on December 17, 1903.

What's the Palooza?

Get your head in the clouds and fly. Wilbur and Orville Wright thought about flying night and day. They spent hours watching birds, particularly buzzards, while trying to figure out the trick of it. They noticed that the birds seemed to twist their wings at the tips. They puzzled over how the stiff wings on the prototype airplanes they were building could possibly do this. Wilbur stumbled on what was to become the Wright brothers' greatest contribution to airplane design: wing warp. He realized that if the wing ends were flexible, they could be twisted or "warped" by a system of cables and pulleys. Today airplanes used hinged surfaces called ailerons to do the same thing. And it all started with two little blokes who dreamed of nothing but flying.

Flying Dreams

Lie on your back on a blanket or a lawn chair on a bright day, with a sky full of clouds. Take a good, long look at the clouds and try to imagine the sky Orville and Wilbur stared up into, before it was filled with planes and other flying machines. They were just dreaming of what might be possible. Now we *know* what it feels like to plow through those fluffy, white pillows in a steel-tipped 747 passenger jet, smoothly cruising at 550 miles per hour! Think about being one of those big birds—a falcon or a hawk or an eagle—with your strong wings spread as far as they can go, slicing through the clouds, free as, well, a bird! There's no better way to daydream than staring at the clouds and thinking about flying.

Now think about your night dreams. Have you ever dreamed you could fly in your dreams? It is one of the strongest, most appealing images to appear in dreams, with you, the dreamer, in flight. When you fly in your dreams, are you flying high in the air, in the clouds, soaring way above everything going on below? Many dream analysts believe that means you have a sort of fearless ambition and a great sense of your own freedom. Or do you fly low to the ground, gliding just above it all? This is said to mean you have reasonable, attainable goals and a solid sense of well-being. Some people don't actually fly in their dreams, but rather take long, flightlike swooping steps that propel them along. This dreamer is said to be finding his independence, and striving to reach his potential. Next time you dream you are flying, when you wake up, try to describe your dream to someone. Or draw it. Try to show or explain how it felt when you were flying, what you could see, how far you flew—and whether you were flying toward something or away from something! Airplanes are nifty, but it's nice to have a great imagination that lets you fly inside your own head.

Build a Fleet

Making a paper airplane is easy. Making a fleet of paper airplanes is awesome. Create your own air force, with different types of planes for different purposes. There are cargo and passenger transports, fighter planes, reconnaissance or spy planes. Use two or three basic paper airplane designs and make

Make It Simple

- - - - - - -

All you need is a piece of 8½-by-11-inch paper and a few paper clips. Here's world-famous paper airplane expert Ken Blackburn's simple formula for a basic airplane that *will* fly!

1. Fold your paper in half lengthwise, creasing carefully.

2. Fold one corner from the top to the center crease.

3. Fold the other corner from the top to the center crease.

4. Reverse your center fold so the creased corners are on the outside.

5. Fold one wing down an inch or so from the center fold.

6. Fold the other wing down so that it's even with the first.

7. Fold the wings out to the side, and add paper clips to the nose (three small or two large clips).

8. Bend the back corner of each wing up a little bit.

9. Throw your airplane gently forward. Make adjustments using another paper clip on the nose or by fiddling with the amount you bend the back of the wings up.

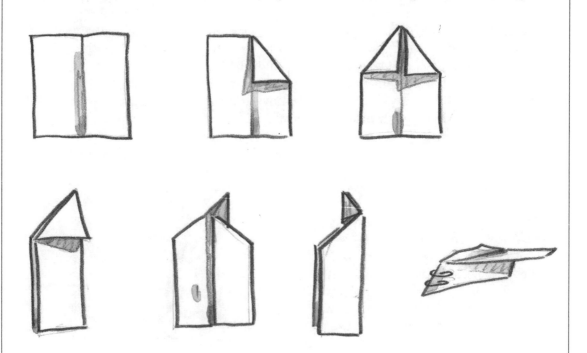

dozens of planes for your air force. Use markers to decorate them to make them look important or fierce or powerful. Give the types of planes names, like the Mustang, Spitfire, Marauder, or Gooney Bird from World War II.

You can also make a fleet of airplanes for your own commercial-style airline. Make big passenger planes or little commuter puddle-jumpers. Name your airline, design a logo and a color scheme, and decorate all your planes with markers. When you're done making your fleet, hang each plane with invisible fishing line from the ceiling in your room. Like I said, awesome.

Invent a Flying Machine

The Wright brothers weren't the first people to imagine what a flying machine might look like. Four hundred years earlier, artist Leonardo da Vinci drew a very realis-

Great Flight Flicks

Around the World in 80 Days

Dumbo

Peter Pan

Chitty Chitty, Bang Bang

Fly Away Home

The Right Stuff

Apollo 13

Make It a Party!

Invites: Decorate your invites with pictures of flight greats like Orville and Wilbur, Charles Lindbergh, Amelia Earhart, Chuck Yeager, even Snoopy and the Red Baron. Include a bit of biographical info about the aviator so your guests can shine in a game of aeronautical trivia at your party. Or feature pictures and info about great airplanes like the *Spirit of St. Louis,* the Wright brothers' *Flyer,* or the Concorde.

Food and Decor: Loads of paper airplanes hanging from the ceiling. Mom and Dad wearing grease-monkey jumpsuits, bomber jackets, goggles. Background tunes might include the sound track from *2001: A Space Odyssey,* or rousing cuts from Frederick Fennell's *Marches I've Missed,* including "Off We Go into the Wild Blue Yonder." Serve peanuts and pretzels in little home-decorated airline-style bags. Little jelly sandwiches wrapped in wax paper, like Lindy ate as he flew across the Atlantic. Airplane-shaped gummies or sugar cookies shaped like planes.

Activities: Make paper airplanes, or fleets à la palooza. Or give everyone easily assembled balsa planes. Then race 'em! Prizes for Distance, Best Crash and Repair, Best Decorated, Best Name, and Highest Flyer. Take turns flying a remote-controlled plane outdoors.

Favors: A balsa or Styrofoam plane, astronaut ice cream, flight wings, goggles.

We could hardly wait for morning to come, to get at something that interested us. That's happiness.

—Orville Wright
(1871–1958)

tic version of what we call a helicopter in his notebook. People still try to dream up new ways to fly; airplane engineers invent experimental airplanes meant to test new concepts or technology. These planes can be mighty unusual looking, and are flown by very experienced pilots who test the planes and then report back to the engineers what worked and what didn't on the plane.

Invent your own flying machine. Dream up a futuristic—or prehistoric!—contraption. Is it long and lean, or stubby and muscular? Does it look like an animal or a building transformed into something that flies? Think about what features will help or hinder your machine's chances for successful flight. Draw it or build it with anything you can get your hands on, such as paper, cardboard, rubber bands, Legos, and so on.

Good Books

Read Russell Freedman's *The Wright Brothers: How They Invented the Airplane,* a wonderful biography with rare photos and lots of juicy bits from the Wright brothers' own notes and journals. Check out *The Wright Brothers for Kids: How They Invented the Airplane, with 21 Activities Exploring the Science and History of Flight,* which tells the Wright brothers' tale, as well as those of other early flight pioneers, and has terrific hands-on activities that explore the principles of flight. And don't forget Ken Blackburn's *Kids' Paper Airplane Book,* a great beginner's guide to making snazzy paper airplanes.

Greetings

Holiday cards are great, but how about skipping the sign-and-send, store-bought greeting cards and celebrating the season with an original impression instead?

What's the Palooza?

Make and send your own custom greeting cards. To keep it simple, you can just draw a seasonal picture and feature it on the outside of a card the way store-bought cards do. Draw your picture on the bottom right quarter of a plain sheet of white paper. Make photocopies of your drawing, then fold each copy like this: Fold the paper in half, turning the top half of the paper to the back. Then fold this in half so your picture is on the cover and the card opens to the right. Use crayons or markers to add a dash of color to your picture. Write a greeting message inside—anything from a simple "Happy New Year!" and your signature to a longer note with holiday news.

If you have the time, you can skip the photocopying and draw original pictures for each card. Give a title to each picture—a picture you've drawn of yourself ice skating might be called *Ice Angel.* Or a picture of your family with their feet up in front of a cozy fire might be called *Toasty Toes at Home.* Don't forget to sign your name and date each piece of art—they are originals!

You can also skip the traditional folded card and use a whole sheet of paper. Write a poem and decorate it around the edges. Your poem can be a sweet little holiday squib or a wintery musing. Or try the "A is for . . ." style, to give yourself a fun prompt: "A is for Angels I make in the snow." Use every letter of the alphabet to describe something you like about winter or the holiday season. Illustrate some or all of your ideas in the mar-

---

Who can play?
Ages 6 and up.

What do we need?
Plain white letter-sized paper, butcher paper, potatoes and washable paints or stamp pads, markers. Access to a computer and printer. Outtakes of family photos. A camera and props. Envelopes of appropriate sizes to hold cards.

Running time?
An hour or two to make cards; extra time for writing short notes and addressing envelopes.

Budget?
$$

gins. You can also write a greeting in haiku form. Or find out how to say "Happy Holidays" or "New Year's Greetings" in a bunch of other languages and cover your card with these exotic words.

One Potato

One of my favorite ways to decorate a custom card is to use old-timey potato stamps, because each card is a rustic, one-of-a-kind piece of art. First prepare the paper you're going to use, either folding letter-sized pieces of butcher paper into card form as above, or cutting the butcher paper into postcard-sized pieces. Now cut a potato in half and pat the flesh dry with a paper towel. Draw a simple design on the flesh with a pencil—a star, a snowflake, a wreath, anything. The simpler the shape, the better. Carefully cut around the shape with a knife (ask a grown-up to help if necessary) to a depth of $1/4$ to $1/2$ inch. Cut away anything that's not a part of your picture. Dry the potato again with a paper towel. Pour a small amount of paint into a shallow dish like a pie plate (you can also use stamp pads). Dip your potato evenly in the paint, careful not to pick up too much paint. Press the potato firmly onto your prepared piece of butcher paper and lift up gently so as not to smudge the image. Let each dry thoroughly before going back to write your messages. Make a few different potato stamps for variety. Or create simple word messages by making potato stamps of different letters—*J, O,* and *Y,* or *S, N, O,* and *W,* for example.

New Year News

You've seen those letters some families send out around New Year's—a long-winded account of everyone's accomplishments and adventures. It's nice to catch up on this kind of family news, but make it more fun by doing it in the form of a newspaper. Dream up a name for your newspaper—the *Smith Sentinel* or the *Annual Dispatch*. My family paper might be called the *Lithgow Ledger!* Write very short "articles" about different family members, headlines and all: "Sue Gets Driver's License—Town on Alert!" The whole article doesn't have to be about one thing; try to load it up with juicy details and funny family news. Depending on how long you want it to be, your newspaper can feature articles, ads, announcements, even a fictional police blotter! Collect a few photographs to use alongside the articles (Sue holding the car keys and grinning). Make a great title logo on the computer for the top of your newspaper. Type up your stories using a newsy typeface—maybe something bold and loud to give it the flavor of a tabloid. If you can scan and place your photos while you're typing the stories and laying out your newspaper, great. If not, just save space for the pictures and glue them in place in the appropriate spot when you print the pages, then make as many photocopies of the whole thing as you need to send out to family and friends.

The Hallmark of a Great Card

In a stroke of classic American ingenuity, an eighteen-year-old man named Joyce Hall took two shoe boxes full of picture postcards and started a business that would become Hallmark Cards, the biggest greeting card company in the world. Back in 1910, on an entrepreneurial hunch, Hall sent bundles of postcards to various general stores in the Midwest, whose customers snatched them right up. He set himself up with proceeds from his postcard peddling, but his real breakthrough was inventing fancy Valentine and Christmas cards that could be mailed in envelopes. Until then, these kinds of greetings were homemade and delivered by hand. As ever, Americans loved a product that would save them time and effort. The cards were a hit, and the greeting card industry was born. Today, more than six billion greeting cards are bought and sent every year.

Photo Op

Use family photos to craft a custom greeting. Pick quirky photos and think of funny captions to go with them. A picture of Dad on a ladder painting the house might have a caption that reads, "The Rembrandt of Raven Road Wishes You a Happy New Year." Scan the picture, type your caption, and print out (or e-mail) a bunch to send. Or glue the picture onto a piece of paper, write your caption below, and photocopy as many as you need. You can also take an ordinary picture of someone in your family and "accessorize" it. Take your boring school picture, for instance, make a bunch of copies of it, and draw a Santa hat and beard on yourself with markers. Or give yourself reindeer antlers and a red nose or a halo and wings. Make each copy a colorful, original card with a funny message.

Instead of a single photo, make a fun collage of family photos to send, leaving an open space somewhere on the page to jot your message. You can also take charge of staging an annual family photo that you send out as a holiday greeting. Forget the snoozy picture of everyone huddled together wearing red sweaters. How about a theme picture that doesn't have anything to do with the holidays? Maybe stage a funny group action shot at the bowling alley or in a raucous game of football. Use props or costumes and stage a photo copying a famous image, like Washington crossing the Delaware, or a famous scene from a movie. The more creative and zany the family picture you take, the more your family and friends will look forward to receiving it every year.

Shortest Day

The winter solstice marks the beginning of the new solar year and the official beginning of winter. So it's sort of like the sun's birthday. Let's help the sun blow out the candles!

What's the Palooza?

Give Christmas, Hanukkuh, New Year's, and Kwanzaa a well-earned rest and offer warm acknowledgment of the winter solstice, which was celebrated by everyone's ancestors, one way or another.

You probably already know that this is the shortest day of the year—you may have noticed it starts getting dark not long after you get home from school! Luckily, it's all downhill from there, because the days begin to get longer starting the very next day. Like a lot of things they didn't understand, our ancient ancestors were both fascinated and freaked out by the solstice. They were fearful of the amount of darkness (no electric lights to keep them company) but awed by the mightiness of it— the power of the sun and their complete dependence on it. Eventually, they created ways to honor and mark the day that were a homage to nature and warmth and light. And so will you.

Who can play?
Ages 6 and up.

What do we need?
Sunflower seeds; dried herbs, leaves, or flowers; a log for burning in the fireplace, a bonfire, or a fire pit; bells.

Running time?
Off and on over the course of the whole day.

Budget?
$

Ring in the Sunny New Year

First find out the exact moment of solstice. Go to the United States Naval Solstice calendar at http://aa.usno.navy.mil/data/docs/EarthSeasons.html to find out the day and hour when the earth is tilted furthest away from the sun. The time can be late at night or early in

The winter solstice occurs around December 22, depending on the solar calendar.

the morning or in the middle of the day. If you're up and about at the moment of solstice, ring a bell to mark the beginning of the brand-new solar year. Even if you can't ring the ritual bell, it's fun to be aware of the time itself—it makes you feel wonderfully in tune with the planet, even just for a minute.

Share the Sunshine

There are lots of great old gift-giving traditions surrounding the winter solstice. One of the best things you can do is give something back to nature. A sweet, simple gesture is to offer a basket of sunflower seeds to your backyard bird friends. You might also make little gifts of nature for the people in your family. Collect lovely objects from the natural world throughout the seasons and make gifts of them on the solstice. A pretty feather, an interesting leaf or seedpod, or a smooth stone to keep on a desk or bureau can be a year-round reminder of our connection to nature. You can also combine bits of nature to make sculptures or objets d'art. A friend of mine collects beautiful stones at the beach and builds

Make It a Party!
- - - - - - -

Invitations: Write your invite on rustic-looking paper—rough at the edges, maybe stained with tea. "Come enjoy our warm Yule log and some Solstice grog!"

Food and Decor: Nature, nature, nature! Decorate with bowls of pinecones and winterysmelling potpourri. String boughs of evergreen over doorways. Hang plain fresh evergreen wreaths. And candles! Serve a yummy grog of warm cider or something eggnoggy. Or invent your own solstice punch and serve it as an annual tradition. Set out bowls of spiced nuts, fruit, cheese, and crusty bread.

Activities: Burn the Yule log (see next page). Have each guest share a story from the previous year about some kindness they were shown, an amazing bit of nature they witnessed, or just something good that happened to them for which they're grateful.

Favors: As each guest leaves, give him a gift of nature, as described above. Smooth, pocket-sized "lucky" stones are a favorite.

little piles of them that remind me of the mysterious Stonehenge in England. You can make small wreaths out of boughs of evergreen or pliable twigs of some winter berry bushes. Keep your eyes open in the outdoors— the treasures to find and share are endless.

Yule Wishes

If you have a fireplace (or a convenient place outdoors to build a family fire), turn out the lights and light up a Yule log (with parental supervision, of course!), which is nothing more than a nice dry oak log burned as a long-standing tradition on the winter solstice. Enjoy the quiet darkness and warm glow of the fire. Make up an elaborate (or modern!) version of the Celtic tale of the Oak King and Holly King. Have each person toss a little bit of dried herbs and flowers into the fire with a good wish for the coming year. As your fire wanes, say a snap-crackly good-bye to the past year. And borrow from an ancient tradition by saving a (stone-cold!) tidbit of wood from the spent fire in a jar or coffee can to use to start next year's Yule log.

The Oak King and the Holly King

According to Celtic mythology, the Oak King and the Holly King battle twice a year over which will rule nature for the next half of the year. These battles take place once at Yule (winter solstice) and once at Midsummer (summer solstice), and invariably the Oak King wins the Yule clash and the Holly King triumphs in the summer. So the Oak King rules over the half of the year that grows lighter, while the Holly King rules over the half that grows darker. The Oak King stands for growth and healing, while the Holly King stands for rest and reflection. But must they fight about it?

Friday-Night Poker

A bowl of popcorn, good pals, and a good hand—what else do you need on a cold Friday night? Not a darn thing, I suppose!

Who can play?
Ages 9 and up.

What do we need?
Fresh 52-card standard card deck, chips (or creative chips substitute, such as paper clips, rubber bands, Legos, and so on), a table big enough for all your players, and snacks!

Running time?
A couple of hours.

Budget?
$

What's the Palooza?

Learn the great American game of poker and get a regular home game going. It's not hard to learn, it's one of the best time-killers ever, and it's a great way to socialize with friends and family. How to play? Someone once told me the best way to learn poker is to watch people who know how to play for three or four games, and then just sit down and join the game. This is also how you'll learn all the great variations of the game you've heard so much about—from Texas Hold'em to Alligator Stud to Chicago. You'll make a few goofy mistakes at first, but you'll be in the swing of things before you know it. To give you an idea of how the game works, here are the basics:

Most poker games are played with a standard 52-card deck. As you probably know, the cards are ranked in value, from highest to lowest, ace, king, queen, jack, 10, 9, 8, 7, 6, 5, 4, 3, 2. Besides being the highest card in the deck, the ace can also be used as the lowest card, just below 2. In some games, a card or cards can be called *wild,* meaning they can be used in place of any other card in the deck. As you also probably know already, there are four suits of cards—spades, clubs, diamonds, and hearts. No suit is more valuable than another; suit only matters in determining when you have a *flush,* which is a kind of hand where all the cards are the same suit.

The Hand

Each player in a poker game is dealt some number of cards from which he puts together a *hand,* which is the final combination of five cards he uses to try to win a game. Poker hands in any type of poker are valued, highest to lowest, as follows:

five-of-a-kind: Four cards of the same rank, plus a wild card (for example, in a game where 5s have been declared wild, four 7s and a 5). Or three cards of the same rank, plus two wild cards (three 7s and two 5s). Or two cards of the same rank, plus three wild cards (two 7s and three 5s). Or one card of any rank, plus four wild cards (one 7, plus four 5s). Of course, this hand can only be achieved in a game where wild cards are declared.

royal flush: A, K, Q, J, and 10, all of the same suit.

straight flush: Five cards of the same suit in sequence (for example, 3, 4, 5, 6, and 7 of hearts).

four-of-a-kind: Four cards of the same rank (for example, four kings).

full house: Three of a kind and a pair (for example, three 10s and two jacks).

flush: Five cards of the same suit (any five in no particular order).

straight: Five cards in sequence (five cards of any suits).

three-of-a-kind: Three cards of the same rank (for example, three 10s).

two pair: Two cards of one rank plus two cards of another rank (for example, two jacks and two queens).

pair: Two cards of the same rank (for example, two jacks).

ace high: A hand with five mismatched cards, the highest of which is an ace.

poker face, n. phrase: The absence of facial expression.

The Game

You can play with just two people as you get to know the game. But the ideal number of players is at least five, because it means more interesting cards in the deck will be in play in any given game—and because it's usually a little more raucous and fun with more players. More than five players are hard to fit around a table and can limit which kind of poker you can play; for instance, there aren't enough cards in a 52-card deck for seven people to play seven-card stud.

Now about those types of games. There are two basic kinds of poker—*draw* and *stud.* In draw poker, each player draws new cards from the deck after the initial cards are dealt. In draw, your cards are usually dealt *facedown,* meaning all the cards you hold are known only to you. Your facedown cards are also known as *hole* cards. You place your bets after being dealt your first cards and after you draw new cards. In stud poker, you play with only the initial cards you are dealt. Some cards are facedown, and some are *faceup,* on display for everyone to see. You bet after each new faceup card is dealt and after the last facedown card is dealt.

Both draw and stud poker games can involve either five cards or seven cards. And both types can be played either *high* or *high/low.* In a high game, the highest-value hand wins the pot. In a high/low game, the pot is split between the players with the highest hand and the lowest hand.

The Pot and the Bets

The *pot* is the total of all the bets made by all the players over the course of the game. This is what you're trying to win with each hand you play. Betting is what puts the sizzle in poker. Besides the strategy of putting together a winning hand, you develop a betting strategy that's sometimes an expression of your genuine confidence in your hand and sometimes an attempt to trick your opponents into thinking you have a better hand than you do. And that's the fun of it!

What are you betting? Poker chips or paper clips or Legos—anything you can assign different values based on color, size, or shape. So for chips or Legos, one color (traditionally white) for the minimum bet, one color for the maximum bet, one for double the maximum bet. If it's easier for you to think of the values in terms of money, say your minimum chip is worth 25 cents, your maximum chip is worth 50 cents, and your double maximum chip is worth a dollar. Leave the real-money betting for big-bucks slicksters in Las Vegas, though. If you're playing for chips or paper clips, you're playing for fun. If you're playing for real dough, it's easy to forget it's just for fun.

Ante Up

An *ante* is a set number of chips placed in the pot by each player before a hand is dealt. This guarantees that each hand that is played has some minimum value—so that even if every player ends up with a crummy hand, the person with the least crummy hand will win a little something for his trouble. Think of the ante as the price of playing the hand. Decide your ante amount before you play the first hand, and keep the amount consistent throughout the game.

The Language of Betting

There are different numbers of *betting rounds,* depending on the kind of poker you're playing. In each round, the bets are made moving clockwise around the table, and each player can either *check, call, raise, or fold.*

When you *check,* you stay in the game but choose not to bet. Once you check, you give up your right to raise the bet during that round. After someone makes the first bet of the round, the other players can only call, raise, or fold.

What's the Deal with the Dealer?

The dealer is kind of the boss of any given game. He decides which kind of poker will be played during that game, he decides whether there will be any wild cards, he establishes whatever quirky rules he wants to, and he monitors the betting, making sure everyone antes up and places their bets properly. Oh, and he also deals the cards! In some poker groups, players take turns being the dealer. Other groups stick with one person who is comfortable dealing and everyone agrees is good at it. A good dealer keeps the game moving and makes sure everyone is playing fair.

When you *call* (or *see*) a bet, you match the most recent bet and place the correct number of chips in the pot. When you *raise,* you match the most recent bet and increase the bet by some amount. After a bet has been raised, all the remaining players in the round have to either call (match) the higher bet, raise it again, or fold. In most poker games, the initial bet can be raised only three times in a round.

If you don't think your hand is good enough to win, you can decide to *fold,* or drop out of the hand. The amount you bet suggests how certain you are that you have a winning hand. You can also *bluff,* that is, bet aggressively to trick the other players into thinking you have a winning hand so they will fold and you can win the pot with your average hand.

Let's Play!

The easiest game to start with is five-card draw. Everyone antes up, and starting with the player to his left, the dealer deals each player one card at a time, facedown, around the circle until each player has five cards.

Tiebreakers!

If two hands in the game are tied in rank, here's how to decide which hand wins:

If two players both have straight flushes, flushes, or straights, the highest card of each hand determines the winning hand. (For example, the hand with a flush high card that's a jack beats the hand with a flush high card that's a 9.) If the highest card is the same in both hands, the next highest card determines the winning hand.

If two players have a full house, the highest three-of-a-kind determines the winner.

If two players have three-of-a-kind, the highest three-of-a-kind is the winner.

If two players have two pairs, the highest-ranking pair in the two hands determines the winner. If both hands have the same high-ranking pair, the lower-ranking pairs are compared, and the hand with the highest lower-ranking pair is the winner.

If two players have a single pair, the highest-ranking pair wins. If both hands have the same high-ranking pair, the hand with the highest-ranking single card wins. If it's still a tie, the next-highest-ranking single card determines the winner.

The players look at their cards, then the player to the dealer's left announces whether he will *open* the betting (make the first bet) or *check* (decline to bet). Moving clockwise around the table, each player announces whether he will *call* (match) or *raise* the previous bet—or if his hand is really awful and/or the betting has gotten too steep, he might *fold*. When the betting round is over, every player is allowed to discard up to three cards and draw three new ones. The person who opened the betting in the first round is the lead bettor in the second round. He can either bet or check to the player on his left. Betting continues as above, moving around the table, until everyone has bet, called, and raised as high as they're going to go—or folded. Now everyone who hasn't folded shows their cards faceup on the table, and the person with the hand of the highest value wins. Play a lot of five-card draw until you've learned all the hand values and have figured out the basic rhythm and strategy of betting. Then try five-card stud. Two cards are dealt facedown and three faceup, with betting taking place each time a new card is dealt. This is fun because you can see some of the cards in each person's hand but have to guess how good the cards are that you can't see. Seven-card stud is played the same way, except each player is dealt seven cards and has to make the best five-card hand he can.

ace in the hole, n. phrase: A hidden advantage kept in reserve until needed.

LOOK

for more of John Lithgow's outrageous and original ideas for inventing your own fun!

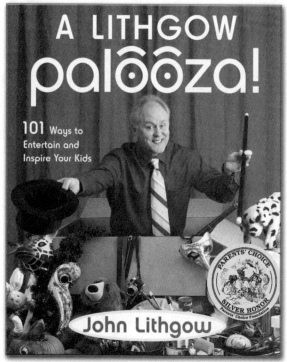

A LITHGOW
palooza!

101 Ways to
Entertain and
Inspire Your Kids

John Lithgow

0-7432-6124-0